The Chrysalis of Religion

A Guide to the Jewishness of Buber's *I and Thou*

S. Daniel Breslauer

Abingdon
Nashville

THE CHRYSALIS OF RELIGION:
A Guide to the Jewishness of Buber's *I and Thou*
Copyright © 1980 by Abingdon

Library of Congress Cataloging in Publication Data

BRESLAUER, S. DANIEL
   The chrysalis of religion.
   Includes bibliographical references and index.
   1. Buber, Martin, 1878-1965. Ich und du. I. Title.
B3213.B83I233   181'.3   79-20067

ISBN 0-687-08040-1

Gracious acknowledgment is made to *Hebrew Studies* for permission to reproduce material that appeared in *Hebrew Studies* 19:8–15 and to the Central Conference of American Rabbis for material that appeared in the *CCAR Journal* (Winter 1978), 27–35.

Quotations from *I and Thou* by Martin Buber, translated by Walter Kaufmann, are used by permission of Charles Scribner's Sons. Copyright © 1970 Charles Scribner's Sons.

Excerpts from *On Judaism* by Martin Buber are reprinted by permission of Schocken Books Inc. Copyright © 1967 by Schocken Books Inc.

Excerpts from *Israel and the World: Essays in a Time of Crisis* by Martin Buber are reprinted by permission of Schocken Books Inc. Copyright © 1948, 1963 by Schocken Books Inc. Copyright renewed © 1975 by Schocken Books Inc.

Quotations from *The Prophetic Faith* by Martin Buber, translated by C. Witton-Davies, are reprinted by permission of Macmillan Publishing Co., Inc. Copyright 1949 and renewed in 1977 by Macmillan Publishing Co., Inc.

MANUFACTURED BY THE PARTHENON PRESS AT
NASHVILLE, TENNESSEE, UNITED STATES OF AMERICA

Contents

To the memory of my father
Daniel Joseph Breslauer
June 10, 1912—April 22, 1964

"The final limit of time . . . is surely the
threshold of eternity."

Buber, *A Believing Humanism*

Preface

When I first began teaching courses in philosophy and religion, the introductory survey usually included selections from *I and Thou* as being representative of a modern Jewish thinker. Because *I and Thou* seemed so devoid of specifically Jewish elements, I was restless with this choice. At first it seemed best to substitute another more explicitly Judaic author—Abraham Heschel, Franz Rosenzweig, or Richard Rubenstein—in the course. Buber's ideas, however, are central for any discussion of modern thought; their relevance is pervasive rather than parochial. Buber's value far exceeds his Judaism. On these grounds one would want to include *I and Thou* for its own sake.

Still the question of Buber's Judaic significance is important. As I taught courses in "Modern Jewish Thought," it became clear that Buber made no division between his Judaic and general thinking. His work presents a total pattern. This situation led me to rethink the meaning of *I and Thou*. Certain themes seemed predominantly Jewish—Buber's explanation of the cult, his focus on idolatry, his recognition of life's duality. Hasidic stories, in his retelling, seemed intrinsically linked with these themes. *I and Thou* could appear as an introduction to these themes which would find fuller expression in Buber's explication of Hasidism. From this premise I developed a sensitivity to the Judaic elements imbedded in *I and Thou*. After a time I became aware that certain parts of *I and Thou* were central to Buber's view of Judaism. *I and Thou,* it seemed to me, set the stage for Buber's special type of Zionism, for his biblical studies, for his interpretation of Jewish religiosity. These discoveries provided the stimulus for this book.

While my experiences in teaching provided the first impetus for writing this book, a more personal stimulus was also involved. During the academic year 1976–1977 I participated in a seminar on Religion and Modernity held at Princeton University. Although I profited from that year I was disappointed to discover that Professor Malcolm Diamond was on leave for the year. I had learned much from his books on Buber and on contemporary religious philosophy. Fortunately I remained at Princeton for 1977–1978. During that time I had occasion to discuss my views with Professor Diamond and to receive invaluable encouragement and criticism. His comments and review of many of the ideas found in this book were helpful not only in shaping the book but in initiating it as well.

My wife as well was inspired by Professor Diamond to explore Buber's work more fully. She aided me by her own interest in Buber, in her demand that I simplify and clarify my own interpretation of Buber's writings, in her recognition of how much I had gained from Buber, and in her support of my work. Her comments helped refine the style and sense of this book.

During the first term of 1977–1978 I taught a class at Princeton University on the Judaic tradition. I found the students a pleasure and challenge to work with. Since a study of Buber was included in the course I found an opportunity to discuss and deepen my understanding of his work. The stimulation from that discussion aided in the writing of this book.

I hope this work will be useful to those who, like myself, find *I and Thou* a stimulating introduction to modern religious philosophy and who intuit its Judaic significance without being able at first to make that explicit. I hope students will find this book a useful companion to their reading of *I and Thou,* increasing their grasp of its concepts and expanding their sense of how those concepts can be applied to one particular religious tradition. I hope that those who, like my wife, find in Buber a congenial exponent of modern Judaism will discover their pleasure in Buber's personal magnetism and intellectual

influence deepened by a study of his philosophical presuppositions. Finally I hope that scholars can find in this book a guide to
the Judaism which Buber sought to establish. Although relating
that clearly idiosyncratic Judaism to *I and Thou* may not establish
its authenticity, it will demonstrate the continuity of Buber's
Judaic concern, even in this very general work.

I gratefully acknowledge the help and inspiration I received
from those mentioned above. I also want to thank Professor
James Woelfel of the University of Kansas for his comments and
careful help in editing the manuscript. I am, of course, solely
responsible for the final form of this book and the ideas expressed
herein.

S. Daniel Breslauer

Introduction

It is hardly surprising that Martin Buber's Jewish credentials need to be established. A number of writers claim that his views are either close to those of Christianity or particularly attractive to Christians rather than Jews. Maurice Friedman even reports that a theological student once asked him, "Professor Buber is so good. How is it he's not a Christian?"[1] Although buried, Buber's Judaic roots are discernible in his use of Hasidic stories, his references to the Hebrew Bible, his concern with specifically Jewish thinkers such as Franz Rosenzweig or Hermann Cohen (see Glossary). His more explicitly Jewish statements—his studies "on Judaism" and his "Zionist" writings—leave no doubt that Buber addresses the world from a Judaic base. In his philosophical writings, however, Buber's Judaism is surrounded by an ecumenical array of material drawn from other world religions. Buddhist, Taoist, and Persian mythology hold honored places in his essays. The Judaic elements are often swallowed or engulfed by Buber's wide-ranging philosophical and universalist approach.[2] The impression that Judaism is but one illustrative example in the midst of any number of equally significant ones may be conveyed if one restricts one's attention to philosophical discussions. Nowhere is that danger more apparent than in the reading of *I and Thou*. While often studied as an example of "Modern Jewish Thought," *I and Thou* contains even fewer references to Buber's Judaism than his other works. Even

9

Buddhist and Christian texts find a more prominent place in this book than do Jewish ones! *I and Thou* contains no mention of Zionism, of Jewish history or literature, of Hasidism, or any other specifically Judaic concern. Taken by itself there would be no grounds to argue that the author of *I and Thou* was a Jew.

The ambiguous content of *I and Thou* presents a problem because *I and Thou* has been seen so often as a representative text of contemporary Jewish thinking. The unmistakable Jewishness of Buber's life and interests together with his other writings has influenced the perception of *I and Thou*. If *I and Thou* is to be considered as a Judaic work, however, it must stand on its own without a reflected Judaic aura. Can *I and Thou* be decoded as a Jewish text? Is it, as Walter Kaufmann says, "steeped in Judaism . . . one of the great documents of Jewish faith"?[3] That question is the central one faced in this essay, but its answer must be given in an unconventional way. Buber's approach to Judaism was idiosyncratic. He refused to allow the "normative" definition of Judaism to constrict him. Jewish law, tradition, and synagogue life provided building blocks but not rigid standards. His Jewishness grew out of but expanded far beyond the conventional Judaism of his time and context. How, then, can his work be decoded as Judaic? Certainly not by comparing it to some essence or distillation of classical Judaism.

The approach advocated here is that of taking Buber seriously when he speaks about the "Jewish soul." Let us allow Buber to guide us to an understanding of Judaism. How does Buber reconstruct Judaism, how does he envision its inner life, its history, its external manifestations? To discover how Buber reconstructs Judaism, the entire corpus of his writings needs to be examined. His statement that "I can describe what has happened to me only as a process of clarification, but not a conversion" must be taken seriously.[4] Both the early and later writings on Judaism, Zionism, and Hasidism need scrutiny. What appears as a hint in one passage receives fuller treatment in another work. As we examine Buber's Judaic writings his visionary perspective comes into focus. Judaism is a promise for the future, a possibility waiting to be realized rather than an actuality already prepared and completed. Judaism is a challenge to which the individual must respond. *I and Thou* should be understood as providing the general context in which the challenge of Judaism is issued. *I and Thou* prepares the way of Buber's Judaism by focusing on those issues and problems for which his reconstructed Jewish religiosity is a solution. *I and Thou* is profoundly Jewish because at its heart is a sensitivity to human dilemmas, a sensitivity which Buber associates specifically with Jewish religiosity.

I and Thou is more than an articulation of those challenges to which Judaism is an explicit response; it does more than bring to the surface the implicit stimuli which lie buried in Jewish religiosity. *I and Thou* provides Buber with an interpretive tool, a hermeneutic, by which he can discover in the Jewish past just that religiosity which his intuition had led him to expect. *I and Thou* is a prologue and a legitimation of Buber's retelling of biblical texts, Hasidic tales, rabbinic anecdotes, and other Jewish myths. What appears utopian and idealistic at first in Buber's approach to Zionism is justified by the politics of *I and Thou.*

Whether as an interpretation of Judaism or an articulation of the presuppositions of Jewish religiosity, *I and Thou* has an intimate relationship with Buber's view of Jewish religion. Before analyzing the book, then, the nature of that Judaism needs to be explored. The nineteenth and twentieth centuries—particulary in Germany and Eastern Europe—saw a proliferation of interpretations of Judaism. No one normative view prevailed, and any attempt to state the essence of Judaism was inevitably subjective, often arbitrary, and clearly a personal statement of faith rather than an objective scholarly summary of fact. Buber's views on the nature of Jewish religiosity are of importance in this study precisely because they reveal so intimately his personal, subjective response to Judaism. *I and Thou* is Jewish not because it is built upon some abstract, ideal Judaism, but because it reflects Buber's vital, if subjective, response to the need for a modern Jewish religiosity.

11

THE CHRYSALIS OF RELIGION

Buber's Reconstruction of Judaism

The Jewish consciousness revealed in *I and Thou* is self-consciously subjective. Buber admits that his Judaism does not coincide exactly with that which many Jewish authorities consider "normative." Buber, however, is interested in discovering the truth of Judaism, its inner meaning. Such a meaning arises for him out of a subjective encounter with the tradition itself. Buber's own encounter with Hasidism, a modern Jewish mystical movement, provides an example of his creative approach.

In the eighteenth and nineteenth centuries a popularly supported mystical movement arose among Jews in Eastern Europe. Its followers called themselves "Hasidim," or "pietists," appropriating a name that had been used by religious extremists from biblical times through the middle ages. The movement itself was called Hasidism. As a social and intellectual phenomenon Hasidism developed an intricate leadership pattern as a rival and alternative to the traditional rabbinic authorities. It evolved new interpretations of Jewish law, ritual, and prayer. A vast literature comprised of biblical commentaries, philosophical studies, talmudic interpretations, liturgical devotions, and folklore and myth was produced by Hasidic leaders.

Martin Buber undertook to reconstruct the religious element buried underneath this mountain of literature. Hasidism was an important witness to Jewish religiousness: "In Hasidism," he commented, "I see merely a concentrated movement, the concentration of all those elements which are to be found in a less condensed form everywhere in Judaism. . . ."[5] Buber distilled these elements from Hasidic myths and folklore. Not only did he sift and condense the material, his artistry transformed it as well. His retelling of Hasidic tales is a refocusing of the original. Through the Hasidic tale Buber reveals his view of Judaism; the tales he retells become restructurings of Judaism.

The central fact of Buber's Judaism is man's task. Hasidism and Judaism in general provide human beings with the key to meaning in their lives. Jewish texts are guideposts pointing the way for persons struggling with the purpose of being. "The task of man, according to hasidic teaching," Buber explains, "is to affirm for God's sake the world and himself and by this very means to transform both."[6] There are four elements which comprise this definition of the Jewish tasks: (1) affirming the self, (2) affirming the world, (3) for the sake of God, and thereby, (4) transforming both. Each of these elements needs explanation: What does it mean to affirm the self? How does one affirm the world? What content do we give to "for God's sake"? And finally, what type of transformation is involved? Answering these questions we discover Buber's Judaism.

Affirmation of self and world means declaring their basic unity and wholeness. The self is affirmed as a whole, complete individual. The world is affirmed as a "cosmos," an integrated totality. The divided person cannot affirm "himself," but only this or that characteristic or "virtue" which he finds within him. A divided universe—whether pluralistic or dualistic—can never be affirmed as a cosmos: it is either condemned in part or exalted in part. What Buber sometimes calls the "two foci of the Jewish soul" are the twin attempts to unify the self and to make the world into a cosmos. The first task is born out of the challenge arising in the individual. Challenged by a transcendent unity—God—the individual discovers that he must respond as a total unified being. Man's relationship to God, the Eternal One, demands that man himself become one. The second task is a social one. The messianic ideal instills in the Jew a sense of the world as incomplete. Society is becoming, but not yet, organic community. Under the messianic ideal all social life is judged and found lacking. The human world is not yet an integrated cosmos. Jewish religiosity, then, demands two things, first "the immediate relationship to the Existent One and second, the power of atonement at work in an unatoned world."[7]

Affirmation of self, that is, the task of unifying one's inner being, is for Buber a major characteristic of Jewish religiosity. The Jew more than any other member of the ancient world experienced his own inner contradictions. Characteristically, according to Buber, the Jew felt the inner division of his soul and was pained by it. In struggling with his personal sense of plurality the Jew discovered the unity of God. Buber adds that the same sensitivity is responsible for the messianic ideal: "Striving to evolve unity out of the division of his I, he conceived the idea of the unitary God . . . striving to evolve unity out of the division of the world, he created the Messianic idea."[8] The sign of a Jew is his concern for unity and his sensitivity to disunity. Because he is profoundly aware of inner self-contradictions, the Jew senses an ideal unity in God; because he is troubled by social divisiveness, the Jew recognizes a divine plan leading to social integration and harmony.

Hasidism reveals Judaism at its most sensitive. Hasidic anecdotes, again as Buber retells them, provide examples of a religious sense of man's inner conflicts together with a transcendent demand for unity. Buber records that he was uneasy when he first heard tell of a certain Hasid, the disciple of the Rabbi of Lublin. The Hasid sought to fast from one Sabbath to the next. For six days the fast progressed without temptation. Then on the final day he suffered from a terrible thirst. Unwillingly the Hasid was drawn to the well and compelled to break his vow. By sheer strength of will he overcame this impulse. Turning from the well he felt a surge of pride within himself. Suddenly he recalled the duty of humility. He determined to break his pride and turned back to the well. Providentially, he no sooner reached it than his thirst vanished, and he could proceed to complete the fast. Buber related his own surprise to discover that the rabbi scolded his disciple: "Patchwork," he declared to the astonished student.[9]

Buber reconciles himself to this parable by noting that the self cannot be unified if it remains oriented to external or internal stimuli alone. The countless demands made by the outside world lead to contradictions and confusions. The numerous voices arising from within the self are equally divisive and distracting. Only a self concerned with a purpose beyond the immediate response to either internal or external demands can become unified. Only a life directed not to this or that goal but to the One God can be made whole. "The Jewish teaching of the wholeness of life," Buber explains, "is the other side of the Jewish teaching of the unity of God."[10] Hasidism, expressive of Jewish religiosity, begins with the divided self because its divisions cannot be reconciled except by turning to God. Judaism begins by recognizing man's inherent disunity; out of this recognition arises a sense of God's unity as the answer and solution to man's dilemma.

Buber has transformed the classical view of Jewish monotheism. Traditionally Jews have claimed to believe in one God, to hold a certain faith about divinity. Buber reverses the process and declares that the Jew begins not with God's unity but man's diversity. Facing the problem of the divided self the Jew is forced to intuit divine oneness. One element in Jewish religiousness—its monotheism—is in fact not a theological principle at all but a response to the human condition. Just as Hasidism enables Buber to transpose an abstract principle— monotheism—into personal reality, so it transforms the other ritualistic and doctrinal elements of Judaism.

Messianism is the polar complement to monotheism in Judaism. Jewish ritual and practice have been interpreted by Jewish mystics as a means of bringing the Messiah. Less mystically inclined thinkers still find in Jewish law and communal structure the blueprint for God's ideal kingdom. Monotheism reveals restlessness about the divided self; Jewish messianism dreams about a perfect society, a community that transcends a divided humanity. Messianic concern for society is interrelated with the monotheistic focus on the self. Buber tells of the Rebbe of Zans who complained that he had reached old age without fully turning to God. He was rebuked and told "You are thinking only of yourself. How about forgetting yourself and thinking of the world."[11] The individual's self-concern here prevents him from even unifying his inner life. Recognizing the unity of God may grow out of man's self-conscious inner turmoil; social strife leads to messianic striving. The individual inevitably discovers that he cannot become a whole person except in community. Yet community itself is divided and fragmented. Individual life develops in freedom, personal choice, and private decision-making. Communal life, however, develops on the basis of structures, rules, organizing principles. Faced with the perplexity of social confusion the individual learns to subsume his own interests under the social good. The Jew is interested in personal unification, but he is not an anarchist. The primary example of pure individualism is that of Korah, the biblical rebel who opposed the authority of Moses. As long as the individual sees himself in oposition to community he remains arbitrary and unfulfilled. Such, Buber suggests, was the fate of Korah. Hasidic writers indicate that redemption will come only when the "soul of Korah is willing to subject itself to the soul of Moses."[12] Affirming the world means affirming that the individual is insufficient to himself. The unity of the world means the communal context of mankind. The Jew, according to Buber, affirms his need of organic social life as well as his need of God. The Israeli kibbutz represents such a Jewish vision. "Whether or not he knows it," Buber writes, "[the Israeli pioneer] is animated by the age-old Jewish longing to incorporate social truth in the life of individuals living with one another."[13]

This age-old longing represents a dissatisfaction with social life parallel to the Jew's restlessness with his own soul. The messianic vision, with its emphasis on obedience to social structures, its ideal of an organic community, grows out of a sensitivity to the problems of institutional life. Monotheism and the messianic ideal are both symptoms of Jewish concern rather than Jewish remedies. The messianic vision responds to the inherent selfishness of men and their antinomian, anarchistic tendencies. No less than monotheism it is a goal born out of a striving against the conflicts found in reality.

Monotheism—the striving after unity of the self—and messianism—the working for a unified world—provide an entrance for God into the human world. God's existence depends upon his being brought into "this world." Affirming monotheism and messianism "for God's sake" entails the declaration that the ideal unity upon which these two strivings depend does not remain aloof in a "supernal world" but is brought into everyday human reality. Buber agrees with Rabbi

16

Hanoch that the difference between Judaism and other religions does not lie in making a distinction between the ideal and the real but in the fact that "Israel professes that the two worlds are essentially one."[14] Without the ideal of a unique God who cares for all mankind neither monotheism nor messianism would be possible. In that sense human beings need God in order to affirm the worth of themselves and of human community. But without monotheism or messianism God's reality would be ineffective in a world divided against itself.

From that perspective God needs human beings. Persons who seek unity of self and society are the means by which God becomes an active agent in human affairs. Self and society are affirmed in this latter case as the means by which the divine works in the human sphere. The answer given by a Hasidic rebbe to the question "Where is God?" resounds in Buber: "God is wherever man lets him in."[15] To affirm self and society for the sake of God means programmatically to dissolve the distinction between holy and profane. If God's presence in human life depends upon the on-going search of every individual for self-unification and all societies for a common community, then every human activity is holy.

Buber is uncomfortable with organized, institutionalized religion because it seems to thrive upon just that dichotomy of holy and profane which Judaism, as he sees it, denies. Individuals, words, behavior, objects are separated from the everyday. Designated as holy they claim a continual, unchanging sanctification. Fragmented limbs, they are frozen in sacredness.

Buber contrasts this static holiness to Jewish religiosity. Religiosity refers to the process by which everyday life is transformed into holiness. The human ability to sanctify a sphere not yet made holy constitutes "the mystery of our existence, the superhuman chance of mankind."[16] The institutions of Jewish life—its holy men, holy books, holy rituals—are for Buber vehicles by which ordinary life is transformed. What is most profoundly Jewish is its religiosity—its way of utilizing institutional religion to enable the individual and community to invest the everyday with sacredness. The contemporary situation,

17

Buber feels, demands that we look beyond Jewish religion to the religiosity for which the religion is but the instrument. Modern need, he suggests, "bids us work for that which is most profoundly Jewish, more Jewish than all forms and all norms: realization, reconstruction of God's community and a new beginning."[17]

Hasidism and Buber's reconstruction of Jewish religiousness focus on this threefold aim—realization of the individual, reconstruction of the community, and the process of beginning again to sanctify the not-yet-sacred. Realization of the individual—theologically expressed as monotheism—means affirming the worth of every individual act as part of a unified, holy purpose, as part of the process of sanctification demanded by the One God to whom all is holy. Reconstruction of God's community—the concrete meaning of the messianic hope—means affirming that universal purpose which binds human beings to a central, living core; it means affirming the purpose of dedicating one's individual power to the fulfillment of the group-ideal, an ideal set by the God who stands for reconciliation among human beings. The process of a new beginning—in his early works Buber calls this religiosity—means a continually renewed drawing of God into the world as an active partner in mankind's effort for personal and social unification. These three tasks are the basis of Buber's view of Judaism, tasks arising from three basic problems: the conflicted self, social contention, and religious stagnation. *I and Thou* confronts precisely these three problems.

I and Thou *as a Prologue to Judaism*

Judaism, as Buber viewed it, perceived three basic problems facing mankind—a psychological dilemma, the divided self; a sociological challenge, the creation of community; and a religious issue, the tension between innovation and structure in religions. *I and Thou* addresses itself to each one of these concerns; it begins with the individual and his predicament and then moves on to consider social life. Only in its third section are specifically religious matters discussed. This third section, however, has colored the way in which the entire book is perceived. Readers expect the book to be a theological tract from beginning to end.

One need only recall the depth of Buber's influence on psychology to realize the injustice of such an approach. In his dynamic relationship with a variety of psychological methods, Buber returns again and again to the views found in *I and Thou*.[18] To emphasize only the psychological relevance of this work, however, is also misleading. Psychology helps Buber construe one, but only one, of the three problems around which the book is focused.

Our survey of Buber's Judaism will provide a clue to the structure of *I and Thou*. The book is diagnostic. It reveals to modern man just those three primal diseases for which Judaism prescribes the antidote. In itself *I and Thou* is not complete. Without Judaism it remains only half fulfilled: we become aware of our problems but do not know how they are to be solved. Looked at from this perspective *I and Thou* gains in meaning. Of course it does not provide all the answers to the questions it raises. It is often allusive and points beyond itself. Before decoding its allusions, however, we can stop to demonstrate how *I and Thou* can be read as the diagnostic prologue to Buber's Judaism.

Monotheism is Judaism's response to the problem of the divided self. *I and Thou* opens with an invitation to perceive man's inevitable conflict, the divided existence which inexorably characterizes his life. Men inescapably live two different forms of existence. Each mode invariably gives way to the other, leaving men dual in their existence. At times we *experience* reality; the world appears as an object to be manipulated. External things are analyzed, defined, set at a distance and utilized as alien, non-self, and other. The self stands over against the non-self, defines its nature in contrast with others. Existence is a battle, a competition, a facing away from all that is not the self. At times, however, men enter into *relationship* and respond to the other (both human and nonhuman) as a partner in living. At such times reality is perceived as a unity of existence in which the self and non-self participate in a broader realm of being. Intimations of wholeness and organic oneness are the residue from these encounters, these relationships. *I and Thou* repeats the theme of duality, of divided being, of man's melancholy fate again and again. Significantly, Buber provides these two realms with names, he gives them a tangible reality by concretizing their existence: the realm of experience is called "I-It," the realm of reciprocity is "I-Thou."

Judaism presupposes a sensitivity to the conflict human beings encounter in reality. *I and Thou* acts as a prologue which makes this inevitable duality a conscious one. Buber's Judaism comes to the fore not as a traditional quotation from a classical text but as the basis upon which he points to

> the sublime melancholy of our lot that every You must become an It in our world. However exclusively present it may have been in the direct relationship—as soon as the relationship has run its course or is permeated by *means,* the You becomes an object among objects, possibly the noblest one and yet one of them, assigned its measure and boundary.[19]

The Jew presumes conflict because he has experienced his own divided ego. Buber universalizes the Jewish experience. All men have a divided ego and can be made conscious of this inner disunity. Persons become selves through the cycle of I-Thou and I-It modes of being. The individual develops self-consciousness first through his relationship with the mother. In infancy the ego takes shape in response to the one who provides all. Awareness of self grows from the midst of an immediate, all inclusive relationship with the protective, enveloping mother (Freud's discussion of the "oceanic feeling" inevitably comes to mind when reading Buber at this point). The child learns to distinguish between himself and his mother; then he discovers that he can use his relationship with her as the basis for manipulation. An instinctive cry for food can be imitated and used to demand attention for its own sake. The child is, as it were, "weaned" from the I-Thou reciprocity of infancy. While the self was formed and developed in relationships, once given an independent existence the self turns to a life of distance and separation. The other who was previously a partner in undifferentiated existence becomes a rival to be manipulated and used to satisfy the interests of the newly born self. The original experience of the child with the mother is paradigmatic. Ever and again the individual grows in self-consciousness through an unmediated relation with another and then utilizes this developed self to place that other at a distance. What was discovered through reciprocity becomes the tool manipulated in I-It living:

> Man becomes an I through a You. What confronts us comes and vanishes, relational events take shape and scatter, and through these changes crystallizes, more and more each time, the consciousness of the constant partner, the I-consciousness. . . .
>
> Only now can the other basic word be put together. For although the You of the relation always paled again, it never became the It of an I—an object of detached perception and experience, which is what it will become henceforth. . . .[20]

Without mentioning monotheism *I and Thou* points to the divided self for which monotheism is the Jewish response. Just as Buber's Judaism moves from monotheism to messianism, so *I and Thou* moves from problems of the self to problems of society. The investigation of the birth of self-consciousness is complemented by a consideration of the human individual surrounded by competing institutions and external pressures. Human beings are coerced by circumstances into culture and society. Defending himself against the onslaught of life's expectations and obligations, the individual seeks refuge in communal organization. The individual turns to others in search of a Thou in expectation of that responsiveness which environmental demands seem to preclude. Yet while the origin of culture and society lies in longing for a Thou, the concrete reality is inevitably I-It. Human society begins as "man's response to his You," and yet "the more powerful the response, the more powerfully it ties down the You and as by a spell binds it into an object."[21] Social divisiveness stems from the conversion of a responsive communal effort into an objective social institution, but such divisiveness is as inevitable as the process itself. Communal life spawns institutional offspring, offspring fated to practice an inevitable parricide.

Fated is the appropriate word. Social life binds human beings to I-It existence. Society which was to have been the refuge from external pressures becomes a bondage of its own. Human life in society becomes a struggle between heteronomy—obedience to imposed law—and autonomy—free submission to one's own self-determined will. Paradoxically the two elements of this struggle imply one another. Human life revolves around both fate and freedom, self-determination and obedience to others. "Fate and freedom are promised to each other. Fate is encountered only by him that actualizes freedom."[22]

Judaism too knows the relationship between obedience and liberty. The freedom of a Korah is unfulfilling; the obedience of a Moses is self-realizing. Jewish messianism provides such a reconciliation of fate and freedom, but *I and Thou* points only to the contradiction and struggle.

Judaism, following Buber's analysis, only begins with the problems of self and society. It affirms them for God's sake and develops a religiosity which transforms the static into the dynamic. *I and Thou,* again as befits a prologue, merely states the paradox. God is found in the realization of the everyday; the Eternal Thou is discovered in relationship: "Extended, the lines of relationship intersect in the eternal You." Paradoxically, however, religion which seeks for God cannot find him. Neither ascetic withdrawal nor enthusiastic earthiness find the divine; "Whoever goes forth to his You with his whole being and carried to it all the being of the world, finds him whom one cannot seek."[23] The problem of religion is that it seeks that which can be discovered only if it is not sought for!

Judaism recognized this problem. It moved beyond religion because it saw the affirmation of the world and the self to be for the sake of God. Buber indicates one solution to this religious

22

dilemma: "You need God in order to be, and God needs you—for that which is the meaning of your life." Stated in such a way, however, God's need for man is a problem, not an answer. It points to the inability of religion to serve the human desire for the divine. Religion answers human need; it places man's response in the center of its program. And very naturally so. Men inevitably seek security, the desire to arrest the passing moment and make it eternal. Men seize the transient and make it permanent (echoes of *Faust!*). Man avoids religiosity and produces religion because he cannot help himself: ". . . we reduce the eternal You ever again to an It, to something, turning God into a thing in accordance with our nature."[24] Jewish religiosity reckoned with man's nature and utilized the forms of religion as a basis for transforming the self and the world. Buber introduces the problem which Jewish religiosity solves as a means of laying the foundations for future developments. *I and Thou* contrasts religion and religiosity and defines the true meaning of idolatry. It does not offer a solution to the problem. It does not reconcile the contrast. *I and Thou* presents Jewish sensitivity, not Jewish religion or even Jewish religiosity. The problem of how religious living can be kept creative lies beyond its scope. Its third section analyzes the inherent contradictions in religion and its forms. This ability to sense the hidden problematics of religion is rooted in that very Judaism about which Buber offers so many cogent discussions in his other works.

I and Thou is a prologue to Judaism. While not yet Jewish religiosity, *I and Thou* establishes the presuppositions and categories which Buber sees as distinctively Judaic. In this sense *I and Thou* is a profoundly Jewish book. More than any discursive exposition of Jewish history, Judaic literature, or Jewish philosophy, *I and Thou* displays the "two foci of the Jewish soul" and the peculiar religiosity which provides the dynamics of Jewish religion. Of course *I and Thou* presents a theoretical structure which implies a drastic reevaluation of the details of Jewish religion. Law and cult, Scriptures and rabbinic texts, all must be read afresh in the light of *I and Thou*. The nature of Jewish worship, the importance of traditional practices, the spiritual dimensions of rabbinic and mystical Judaism, take on new meaning when read with *I and Thou* in mind. In that sense Buber's Judaism is a reflection of *I and Thou*. In another sense, however, *I and Thou* is rooted in and derived from Buber's Judaism. Without the sensitivity which Buber claims is characteristic of Judaism *I and Thou* is unthinkable. Lacking references to the Bible, to rabbinic sources, even to Hasidic writings, *I and Thou* testifies to the power of the Jewish tradition to awaken within one a sensitivity to the spiritual dilemma of being human.

Chapter I

I and Thou as a Jewish Hermeneutic

I and Thou *and the Problems of Jewish Religiosity*

Although *I and Thou* is Judaic in structure and sensitivity, its Jewish relevance extends beyond that rooting in Buber's Judaism. The reader of *I and Thou* misses a deeper level of meaning if the importance of its discussion of religion remains merely abstract and academic. Buber was keenly aware of the dilemmas facing the modern Jew. Behind the wide, general scope of *I and Thou* Buber is constantly directing attention to specifically Jewish problems. *I and Thou* is a document of Jewish religion because it offers a technique by which the most problematic issues of Judaism in the modern world can be confronted. We will look at four of these issues: the sources of Jewish faith, the pattern of Jewish living, Zionism, and the theological dilemma of modernity. The last problem is the only one specifically mentioned in *I and Thou* yet the other three are given an oblique commentary. Applying *I and Thou* to questions of interpretation, religious practice, religious politics, and doctrine will disclose the Judaic relevance which lies below the surface of Buber's philosophical musings.

This investigation will begin by considering the problematics of Jewish literature. Judaism considers action and religious practice more central than doctrine, so it may seem strange to begin with literature. Ever since Baruch Spinoza, however, the question of authority and the relevance of tradition has been connected with exegetical issues. Modern man cannot escape the challenge of Spinoza, and without answering that challenge religion runs the risk of being reduced to mere politics. Spinoza's critique of the Bible can easily be extended to rabbinic literature and later Jewish writings. How *I and Thou* confronts this potential danger will be our first concern.

The Problematics of Jewish Literature

Baruch Spinoza's *Theologico-Political Treatise* proclaims a daring and ambitious goal: to show that "The Bible leaves reason absolutely free, that it has nothing in common with philosophy, in fact that revelation and philosophy stand on totally different footings."[1] While Jewish mystics may have insisted that revelation was a higher source of knowledge than philosophy, they never denied that the Bible addressed philosophical issues, that biblical truth had enough in common with philosophy to criticize it. Jewish philosophers executed difficult exegetical maneuvers to demonstrate how Judaic texts had anticipated and solved philosophic questions of the creation of the world, the reality, power, and attributes of the divine, and the relationship between faith and science. Spinoza's biblical criticism struck at the hidden assumption of these interpretive attempts: that Jewish Scriptures give voice to the word of God that is eternally relevant, everlastingly significant. Spinoza relegated Scriptures to the realm of outdated historical documents. The Bible, according to his view, had authority and meaning only for that society in which it had been created and whose civil mechanisms legitimated it. The validity of such religious writings depended upon two historically conditioned elements: secular legislation and social context. Because Jewish literature became law through its association with the kingship, its authority was limited to the period of the kingdom. Because its goal grew out of the historical context and social needs of the Israelites, its significance was restricted to that particular historical and social period. Biblical laws, Spinoza concluded, "were valid only while the kingdom lasted," and by aiming at "temporal advantages" forfeited their right to be identified with "everlasting divine legislation."[2]

Spinoza's approach undermined the sophisticated exegesis of Jewish philosophy and mysticism. Interpretation became illegitimate if it sought to make an ancient text relevant in modern times. The traditional attempts to reconcile sacred texts and contemporary thinking were as pointless as they were futile. If Scripture was a historical document limited to its particular social context, then efforts, no matter how ingenious, to reveal its "eternal value" were doomed as inappropriate "eisegesis"—a reading into and not out of the text itself. Scripture was deprived of both religious authority—since the source of that authority resided in a now nonexistent kingdom—and religious value— since its original purpose had been pragmatic and sociological. Spinoza recognizes the implications of his view. Jewish law and ritual become inappropriate in modern times. Every human community has laws and rituals, but the only legitimate ones are those enacted by the reigning monarch; all religious practices are "under the sole control of the sovereign power."[3] The modern Jew who takes Spinoza seriously faces a dilemma: can he continue to regard the literary legacy of Judaism as a spiritual resource even if he does not regard its laws as authoritative? Has Spinoza neglected a level of meaning which while neither law nor eternal truth is nevertheless religiously relevant to modern man? A Jew who seeks to affirm the Jewish tradition without ignoring Spinoza's challenge must face that question. Answering it requires a different type of sensitivity both to traditional texts and the problems of modern life than that animating the ancient and medieval exegetes. In short, in responding to Spinoza, the modern Jew engages in the task of discovering a new hermeneutic, a new mode of interpretation to open the closed portals of Scriptural meaning.

I and Thou *as a Hermeneutic*

Biblical scholars and literary critics have questioned Buber's biblical studies. While Buber's basic approach has been appreciated, his specific application of that approach has raised questions.[4] However, critics have neglected Buber's indirect and allusive refutation of Spinoza. While explicit references to Spinoza are almost nonexistent in Buber's writings, his approach to literature represents an authentic response to the type of biblical criticism Spinozistic influence inspired. Not only in his explication of biblical texts, but also in *I and Thou,* Buber uses his theory of art to oppose the Spinozistic reduction of a text and its meaning to one specific historical and sociological context. Buber's aesthetics stand within an important philosophical tradition.[5] In discovering the Judaic implications of *I and Thou,* however, the philosophical question of Buber's roots and influence is not central. The major concern here will be to show how his theory of art enabled a continued relevance for the Bible, rabbinic literature, and later Jewish writings. The exegetical work which Buber produced in order to demonstrate the contemporary meaning of the Bible, midrash and halacha, and Hasidic tales, is grounded in *I and Thou.* How *I and Thou* prepares the way for a new type of interpretation of Jewish literature, an interpretation that refutes Spinoza's claims, is the focus of our investigation.

Buber sets about performing a difficult balancing act: he neither denies that holy writings are products of human beings responding to historically conditioned environments, nor relegates the meaning of those writings to the curiosity of historians. Despite his admission that the Bible and later Jewish texts are human and historical documents, Buber finds within them a witnessing to that which transcends the exclusively human or the merely historical: they testify to the reality of encounter, of meeting. At the very least, an artistic production proclaims its origin in a "Post-Threshold" encounter between man and "spirit." More profoundly, a religious art form gives evidence of man's meeting with "the Eternal Thou." The purpose of the exegete is not merely to sketch in the background and details of the social and historical context surrounding a literary work. Spinoza contends that such socio-political archaeology is the legitimate and sole task of the literary critic. Beyond the boundaries of such investigation the scholar cannot validly venture. Buber rejects this position by requiring that the critic see a literary work as the result of a meeting and the anticipation of a future meeting. An artistic creation is a bridge between two encounters and cannot be understood without giving attention to the two realities joined by that bridge. The meeting—socially and historically conditioned—that gave rise to the text or artistic creation does in fact lie in the past. It is that original encounter which we can reconstruct using Spinoza's methodology. The anticipated meeting in the future, however, is always *about to occur,* always a potential reality. This meeting is one which we in the present must be prepared to enter. An artistic work has modern relevance as a bridge from the past into a future encounter in which we are invited to participate. If a work of art is such an invitation, then despite its origin in a specific historical period, its importance is enduring and continual.

How does Buber construct his theory so that it can move beyond the reductionism of Spinoza? He begins by considering the origin of art. From whence derives the impulse to create artistically? Art originates in the confrontation between a human agent and an ideal waiting to be realized. Art is neither a reproduction of an external reality nor a figment of the artist's imagination. Art derives from the realization of an idea, a form, a being of the spirit, by means of man's ability to transform spirit into corporeal representation:

> This is the eternal origin of art that a human being confronts a form that wants to become a work through him. Not a figment of his soul but something that appears to the soul and demands the soul's creative power. What is required is a deed that a man does with his whole being.[6]

All art—and Scripture as literature is an art form—grows out of an encounter, a relationship. A person responds to the demand of spirit standing over and against him. While executing that demand an artist must, Buber admits, distance himself from his "other"; although the original meeting with spirit occurs in the realm of I-Thou, the act of bringing the form from potential into actualization demands the utilization of a craft, requires skills acquired in I-It living. The artistic creation inevitably shares the historical and social determinacy of its creator. As a historical object it can be analyzed, studied, and dissolved into its component parts. Yet by its very existence it points beyond the historical and social context in which it was created. What originated in encounter can become the basis for a new encounter. "The created work," according to Buber, "is a thing among things and can be experienced and described as an aggregate of qualities. But the receptive beholder may be bodily confronted now and again."[7] The author or artist intended more than he in fact created. That intention informed the historical product with power and significance.

On the basis of this view Buber reexamines the purpose of the interpreter of art or literature. The critic must be attentive to more than the historical or informational relevance of a text or work of art. Interpretation that remains on the level of I-It experience has limited its own ability to comprehend the work's original impetus. Only by bringing the immediacy of encounter to the contemplation of art or literature can an interpreter fathom the depths of its original conception.

Not only is the historian of art or literature misled by a blindness to the encounter which stimulated creativity, but a human opportunity is missed as well. The historian has merely failed to grasp the intention behind a historical document. The reader as human being, however, has forfeited a deeply humanizing encounter in his own personal development. Every artistic creation is an invitation, an occasion to enter the realm of relationship. Buber finds that art is a portal to encounter, a passageway into the I-Thou dimension. The spirit enters man's world and is realized through form, but form is a concession to the categories of I-It. Spirit remains a dynamic "other" hidden in the structure of artistic form. What had once been lived encounter can again become vital meeting. A work of art demands more of its beholder than contemplation, Buber explains; it requires a reconversion back into spirit. Form is man's necessary tool, but it is only a tool. Art demands that man transcend the tool and reach the goal—living relationship. The origin of art lies in spirit become form; the goal of art is form become spirit: "Spirit become word, spirit become form—whoever has been touched by the spirit and did not close himself off knows to some extent of the fundamental fact: neither germinates and grows in the human world without having been sown; both issue from encounters with the other."[8] Art testifies to a depth of being human unknown otherwise. The meaning of art lies in its ability to point to the I-Thou dimension.

Buber mentions two forms that testify to the I-Thou encounter—word and image. Beyond these there is a third that needs consideration which he calls "teaching." Teaching is the fulfillment of spirit in a lived human life. Art and literature are the means by which the goal is conveyed. A life is the end toward which they are pointing. Above image-making or knowledge is a life formed in response to spirit. Encounters with art or literature are stages on the way; meeting with people is the highest aim. All forms—whether imaged or written—aim toward life, toward an individual who realizes their message in his daily being, in his personality. Buber mentions some whose lives are such expressions of I-Thou responsiveness that they become art forms of I-It existence, concrete personalities whose very being is a testimony to man's encounter with spirit: Socrates, Goethe, Jesus. Art has as its *telos* human realization; literature is for the sake of *teaching*. Teaching is not this or that philosophy, this or that system of thought, but a pattern of living—the pattern of responsive reciprocity. Teaching is a continuing human effort seeking the possibility of encounter:

> Here the You appeared to man out of a deeper mystery, addressed him out of the dark, and he responded with his life. Here the word has become life, and this life, whether it fulfilled the law or broke the law—both are required on occasion lest the spirit die on earth—is teaching.[9]

Buber's statement about teaching touches on his approach to religious forms. A life can transcend form for the sake of encounter. Buber's ambivalence to the law—the fact that teaching sometimes fulfills and sometimes denies it—needs close attention. At the least this ambivalence shows an ordered priority of forms. While images, words, and lives are all aspects of existence, the latter are given a higher status. Because of this status the exegete should temper his view of texts with an understanding of lives. The message transmitted by words is supplemental to the message conveyed by action. Teachings complete and explicate the written word.

Recognizing that lives rather than words or images represent "teaching" in its fullest stage, the exegete moves more cautiously when interpreting a text. A Spinozistic concentration on texts and contexts exclusive of human response creates an incomplete view of an author's message. Written texts are afterthoughts, results of an encounter which point to their origin but do not express it. The meaning of the encounter—a meaning that pervades all life—is only palely reflected in the text. Sensitivity to human living rather than literary analysis is the tool by which such texts find their completion:

> The meaning we receive can be put to the proof in action only by each person in the uniqueness of his being and in the uniqueness of his life. No prescription can lead us to the encounter, and none leads from it. Only the acceptance of the presence is required to come to it or, in a new sense, to go from it.[10]

One studies a text in order to respond to it as a total person. Without that response the text remains incomplete and its meaning is lost. Decoding a text means moving beyond its words and structure to the personal testimony behind it and the personal response demanded by it.

If this is true for literature and art in general it is more so for religious art and literature. Religion provides forms by which men indicate that "Eternal Thou" whose presence is intuited in every I-Thou encounter. Social, artistic, and literary testimonies to relationship are only indirect statements about the Eternal Thou; religious forms bear a direct message. They fill out the implicit recognition of an Eternal Thou which other forms convey but do not explicate. Since the Eternal Thou is met only through the dynamics of relationship, religious forms depend upon that same flexibility and transformation back into encounter characteristic of all artistic creations. Religious change is the mode by which these forms are kept vital and open to encounter. The history of religion is the story of forms originally alive with a sense of encounter giving way ever and again to frozen forms which are then renewed with dynamic power:

> The history of God as a thing, the way of the God-thing through religion and its marginal forms, through its illuminations and eclipses, the times when it heightened and when it destroyed life, the way from the living God and back to him again, the metamorphoses of the present, of embedment in forms, of objectification, of conceptualization, dissolution, and renewal are one way, are *the* way.[11]

Religion offers the paradigm case: an encounter demands crystallization in form, the form demands the renewal of personal encounter. Stagnation of form is given a special name in religion—idolatry. Once we comprehend that idolatry is but a specialized name for a general phenomenon—the freezing of form—we can correct a frequent misconception. Buber talks about the changing forms by which men express God. The God-Idea emerges from men's encounters in history. Buber self-consciously looks at the development of the God-Idea from man's standpoint. "Our concern, our care," he alerts the reader, "must be not for the other side but for our own, not for grace but for will."[12] Even with this provision Buber's discussion seems to imply a changing God, an emerging divinity. God takes on shape and is "realized" in the world through the human encounter with him. Not only does man need God, but God needs the reciprocity of man in order to become real in the world of experience. Buber depicts God's "emerging" form, his "becoming" in the realm of experience. A religious text, he suggests, describes that stage of emergence represented by the response of the author to the

Eternal Thou. Religion is the instrument by which the growing conception of God is given concrete existence in human life:

> Ever new regions of the world and the spirit are thus lifted up into form, called to divine form, in the course of history, in the transformations of the human element. Ever new spheres become the place of a theophany. It is not man's own power that is at work here, neither is it merely God passing through, it is a mixture of the divine and the human.[13]

Since Buber speaks of a "mixture" of the divine and human one might be tempted to make God's reality dependent on man. Is Buber talking about a "growing God," whose very nature depends upon the response of his creatures? Read in the light of Whitehead and Hartshorne, Buber can be interpreted as sharing their view of a God whose nature emerges from his contact with creation.[14] But taken in the context of his theory of changing forms and the relationship between spirit and form, such an interpretation of "God's emerging form" can be rejected. The cycle of human religiousness, rather than any statement about the nature of God in himself, is Buber's subject. Buber merely demonstrates that men's views of God are subject to the same round of development, change, and renewal as all other formal responses to spirit. Buber is not speaking theologically but anthropologically. He does not describe God's being but rather man's inevitable way of response. If man's religion is to be creative, if it is to lead ever and again to encounter, then religion must be an expressive, evolving, and emerging portal to reciprocity. A text must be taken as representative of one response, of one limited effort to reduce encounter to form in order to have encounter issue from form.

The Task of the Exegete

In contrast to Spinoza, who confined the task of the interpreter to one goal—illuminating a text in terms of itself—Buber sees four elements in the interpreter's position. He must recover the original confrontation of the author with spirit;

he must himself respond to the spirit found in the form; he must recognize that lives rather than texts are primary; and while dealing with a religious text he must discover the form of the Eternal Thou indicated. The authority of a text is thus intrinsic rather than extrinsic, and he sees the Bible in this way. Religious authenticity depends on creativity, and the religious authority of Scripture resides in its ability to stimulate new forms of relationship rather than in an external authority invested in the text by men in power. Such an exegesis not only deprives Spinoza's historicism of its point, but denies Spinoza's claim that the Bible is a political text and must be understood as such. Our study will look first at the way in which Buber's biblical investigations are clearly refutations of Spinoza based upon the four exegetical principles noted above. Moving beyond Spinoza, Buber's writings on talmudic and rabbinic literature and his creative use of Hasidism can also be understood as growing out of his exegetical concerns. Not Spinoza but other theologians or neo-Hasidic storytellers will be the base of our comparison for these latter writings by Buber—Leo Baeck in the one case and S. Y. Agnon in the other.

Miracles and Prophecy: Two Crucial Issues

In order to refute Spinoza, Buber argued that the meaning of a religious text lies beyond the reach of textual analysis alone. Turning from texts in general to the Bible, Buber's argument becomes especially crucial in two perplexing areas—miracles and prophecy. These subjects are perplexing because they seem alien to modern thinking. While biblical ethics, law, and poetry can all find a response in the modern heart, the claim that miracles verify religious beliefs, that prophets have a private, personal source of truth unavailable to others and the rhetoric of faith which demands surrender to supernatural powers, alienate the enlightened mind. The suggestion that these supernatural fireworks are merely political ploys is certainly plausible. What better way to insure an audience and a receptive hearing than to claim divine approval? How else to invoke authority and demand obedience than to fabricate miracle stories to demonstrate the dire consequences of rebellion? Spinoza offers just these arguments. Miracles are used in the Scriptures, he declares, as a means of keeping the masses in line. Morality is enforced by fear, and miracles promote just such devoted fear. A miracle, clearly, cannot be an actual report about a historical event. No human being could be so mistaken in his scientific investigations as to find the miracle stories even partly credible. The lack of rational support for these tales is evidence enough that they were fashioned out of sheer imagination. Miracles have only one purpose, Spinoza contends: "to excite wonder, and consequently to impress the minds of the masses with devotion."[15] Because the biblical age was one of ignorance and superstition, miracle stories could be effective. Playing off the lack of scientific sophistication in their historical context the biblical writers could perpetrate mass delusions. Defending himself to a critic, Spinoza declares that he finds nothing inconsistent in declaring ignorance and miracles "as equivalent terms." As part of his argument Spinoza notes that the purpose of miracle stories is "not to teach philosophy, nor to render men wise, but to make them obedient."[16]

Buber's response to Spinoza's approach would not take issue with the suggestion that the form in which the miracle stories are couched is the product of a historical period. Certainly authorities did use these stories to insure obedience to a specific legal code. No less than Spinoza, Buber is unwilling to reduce miracle stories to factual reports of historical events. Buber, however, will distinguish between the uses to which a story, perhaps even necessarily, was put and the initiating motive for creating the story. Buber asks two questions: what was the event which the story sought to convey, and why was the miracle form used as the means of communication? Unlike Spinoza, Buber is interested in origins. He seeks to elucidate the wellsprings of miracle narratives. The physical event, even supposing it was an external rather than an internal one, was merely the occasion for the miracle. That event Buber locates within the individual; it was a transformation of self. Miracle language conveys an autobiographical message, that "something happens to us, the cause of which we cannot ascribe to our world." While some who seek to "demythologize" the Bible want to render miraculous language into natural categories, Buber focuses on the unusualness of the language itself. A miracle tale does not seek to describe the supernatural using natural language; it is rather an example of extraordinary linguistic feats. Spinoza finds the language of the Bible calculated to obscure ignorance; Buber finds the language a revelation—it reveals a wonder too marvelous for commonplace words. Spinoza claims that biblical language is a mask hiding natural phenomenon; Buber finds that language describing an internal event which "cannot be grasped except as an act of God."[17] Buber finds in the biblical narrative a self-conscious rejection of ordinary history. The everyday understanding of historical process is judged inadequate. Buber concurs with the biblical writers. There is a nonhistorical, nonscientific level of being. Miracle stories open the way to recognizing this mode of being. To live with a miracle story is for biblical man what openness to I-Thou is for a modern reader of Buber—it prepares a person for encounter:

> The real miracle means that in the astonishing experience of the event the current system of cause and effect becomes, as it were, transparent and permits a glimpse of the sphere in which a sole power, not restricted by any other is at work. To live with the miracle means to recognize this power on every occasion as the effecting one.[18]

In simpler language Buber is saying that a miracle is the recognition of God's power at work. Coupling this biblical commentary with *I and Thou,* we can say that a miracle is an encounter on the I-Thou level with a world that had heretofore been conceived of as I-It. Miracle language points to a recognition of new dimensions of being that exist within, not apart from, everyday reality. The duality of the experience—on the one hand, all is as it always was, nothing has "changed," nothing "new" is added; and yet on the other hand, everything has changed and nothing remains as it was—explains the odd language of Scripture. Of course our "modern" minds are uncomfortable with miracles. The stories were meant to be "uncomfortable." "Miracle is not something 'supernatural' or 'superhistorical' . . . [but is an event] which for the person to whom it occurs, destroys the security of the whole nexus of knowledge for him."[19] Why does the Bible choose to use miracle language?—because that language stuns the mind and challenges the fixed certainty of reason. Biblical style is for the sake of retaining the immediate wonder which becomes static when encased in narrative form. Spinoza used modern sophistication as a critique of miracles. Buber turns this around—the Bible is a critique of all rationalism, including the modern variety! The contemporary reader who finds the Bible difficult reading because of the frequent reference to miracles is taught to take them as a challenge to himself. The Bible demonstrates a "religious *viewing* of history" and demands to be taken as an indication that such a "viewing" is legitimate and possible.[20]

Buber has used his basic exegetical tools—a search for the primal encounter, his emphasis that the individual person rather than a teaching or a chronicle is intended, his contention that the text can awaken responsiveness from the reader, and his glimpse of a "religious" viewing of life—to make the biblical narrative a powerful address to modern man. He suggests that the Jewish Bible, when read perceptively, challenges us to see history in a different way. Modern man cannot accept supernatural legends as if they were historically accurate. Such an approach is intellectually untenable: "If that were the case, man of today in deciding to accept the Bible would have to make a sacrifice of intellect which would cut his life irreparably in two."[21] Such a sacrifice is unnecessary. The Bible provides insight on the world of relationship, not on history. The appropriate reading of the Bible subordinates historical questions to those of encounter, of I-Thou. The text is a key opening up the original encounter, the portal to meeting. The reader is asked to read responsively with the biblical narrative, to challenge himself to hear the words addressed to him through the text. To read this way

38

he must read the Jewish Bible as though it were something entirely unfamiliar, as though it had not been set before him ready-made at school and after in the light of "religious" and "scientific" certainties; as though he has not been confronted all his life with sham concepts and sham statements which cited the Bible as their authority.[22]

Buber asks modern men to read the Bible, not as a historical document to be dissected, but as a living invitation to enter a new realm of being. Spinoza's accuracy as a critic is not in dispute, rather his value as a guide to living religious response and to the Bible as a stimulus for that response. Miracle language seems, after Spinoza, an unpromising entrance into the Bible; Buber refutes this inference and thereby supports his own claim to have discovered a means by which the Bible can be made powerful for modern men.

Modern people are restless not merely with the miracles from the Bible but also with the type of leader described in it. The kings, priests, and secular administrators all seem familiar and recognizable, but the prophets are rather strange. Are they poets, imaginative writers, artists whose vision is dominated by weird dreams? If so, what are they doing in public affairs? Why should they interfere in politics? Are they inspired messengers of God? If so, why are such messages so vague and imprecise? More to the point, if God wants to talk to men that way, why doesn't he speak in our times? Why are prophets restricted to the Hebrew Bible?

Buber responds that prophecy is not as restricted or as esoteric a phenomenon as modern people often think. Buber never goes to the rather popular ploy of pointing out "modern prophets" but he implies that moderns can live out a prophet life-style. Spinoza had condemned the prophets as mere artistic imaginers. The prophet teaches men nothing they would not know otherwise; he merely couches phenomena in simplistic, irrational terms. Buber responds that the prophet's way of phrasing the issues, of drawing attention to something already vaguely sensed, is a genuine achievement.

What is prophecy? Spinoza declares it to be a peculiarly biblical phenomenon—an imaginative presentation of God's laws, justifying those laws by an appeal to supernatural visions, direct contact with the divine, and unusual psychic phenomena. Buber finds prophecy to be an enduring type of leadership—the leader who suggests alternatives, who uses imagination to arouse his audience's ability to choose. Are there modern prophets? Buber would respond in the affirmative: any leader who cultivates his followers' ability to make decisions is prophetic; the leader who places the choice before his people is a prophet. A chain of prophetic leaders stretches from biblical times into the present. Buber's own Zionism provides a prophetic alternative to the dogmatic politics of Theodor Herzl.

This construction of prophecy contradicts Spinoza's attempt to limit the prophetic movement to a certain culture in the ancient Near East. Spinoza felt that prophetic politics was tied to its own time and historical location; it may have been appropriate for primitive Israelites but was ill-suited for modern men. Buber does not deny the political relevance of prophecy but locates the prophetic message in its style rather than its content. While the visions of the prophets were, as Spinoza contended, conditioned by their culture, their mode of placing the choice before the people is—Buber argues—an enduring legacy. Spinoza's critique of biblical prophecy focused on its historical setting and the limitations of the biblical prophet. His critique raised certain questions. If the prophets belong to the biblical period are their words no longer significant? Can the prophetic message be ignored as an anachronism? Can the prophets be dismissed as propaganda and politics and as not essentially religious? Buber places prophecy at the center of modern life. He claims that the modern Jew is the living continuation of prophetic faith. Speaking of Isaiah's confrontation with Ahaz, Buber moves from biblical exegesis to a statement about contemporary Jewish existence:

> We live by that encounter in the highway of the fuller's field, we live
> by virtue of the fact that there were people who were deadly serious

about this *Ha-Melekh* in relation to all of their social and political reality. They are the cause of our survival until this new opportunity to translate the spirit into the reality we have a presentiment of.[23]

Buber's Zionism, intimated here and to be discussed more fully in a later chapter, depends upon the continuation of prophetic faith. Judaism must be founded on the truth and power discovered in prophetic utterances. Without a hermeneutic that can make biblical prophecy creative for modern man, Judaism as Buber sees it cannot survive. Spinoza had condemned the prophetic report as based on imagination rather than reason. The prophet does not possess a "peculiarly perfect mind," but rather "a peculiarly vivid imagination." Studying the Bible can provide psychological insights, it can help us learn about man's imaginative powers; it does not provide truth nor is it useful in man's quest for knowledge. Spinoza points out that even the Bible itself recognizes how dependent the prophetic vision is on its historical context. The visions of Isaiah are different from those of Ezekiel. The cause of that difference lies in their historical context, their personal disposition, their specific training. Prophetic style does not reflect God's revelation "but, according to the learning and capacity of the prophet, is cultivated, compressed, severe, untutored, prolix, or obscure." Spinoza's exegesis makes it difficult to use the prophetic vision as a means of contemporary religious inspiration. The prophet's meaning is inextricably bound to his own context. Historical value may be found through excavating a biblical text, but no other, more personal, worth can be derived from it. A man in search of wisdom, religious truth, or even spiritual enlightenment, is ill-advised to turn to Scripture. While the prophets may teach morality and charity, other philosophies do so more clearly without the imaginative overlay of the Bible. "It therefore follows," Spinoza writes, "that we must by no means go to the prophets for knowledge, either of natural or of spiritual phenomena."[24]

An entire tradition of Jewish eisegesis stands against Spinoza. Jewish interpreters tended to read into the prophets their own ideas of knowledge, truth, and values. Certainly one way in which the prophetic message was kept alive in Judaism was through such "reading into" rather than "reading out of" the text. Either the prophets have clearly stated their intention, Spinoza seems to argue, or that intention is not discoverable. If reason cannot find the message of a passage within that passage itself, then a passage must be declared meaningless. A prophetic message cannot be made contemporary by infusing the contemporary between the ancient lines. Spinoza points out that such an approach renders the Bible susceptible to any meaning—no matter how farfetched—that may be read into it:

> If, again, it is permitted to pretend that the passage has another meaning, and was written as it is from some reason unknown to us, this is no less than a complete subversal of the Bible; for every absurd and evil intention of human perversity could, thus, without detriment to Scriptural authority, be defended and fostered.[25]

The exegete who seeks to restore the present relevance of the Bible must do so without recourse to a "reading in" of contemporary issues. If he seeks to be faithful to the text and not allow any idea whatsoever into his interpretation, the exegete must establish guidelines and criteria. Spinoza's claim is that those criteria must come from the text itself.

Buber does not disagree in principle with Spinoza, but he sees more to a text than the ideas it expresses. He pays particular attention to style—repetitions, key-words, choice of imagery. He notes, for example, in Second Isaiah a constant use of repetition, an equating of the three major themes: creation, revelation, and redemption, a recurrence of similar word patterns in differing contexts. From this he concludes that

> the analogy or even the essential unity of creation, control in history, and redemption imprints itself in the memory of the hearer or reader whose heart is open to receive. Certainly this is no mere artificial means of expression, but the unity of the spheres in the prophet's faith in God transposes itself into a unity of speech and expresses itself in it.[26]

Three elements are intermixed in this passage. In the first place Buber, no less than Spinoza, sees prophecy as pointing beyond empirical fact, as transmitting something other than knowledge. He does not label this "imagination" but remains open to what it might be. He studies the style, the form, the speech of the prophet to rediscover what that noncognitive element might be. Secondly Buber demands of the hearer or reader an openness of heart. Were the message only a cognitive one then an open mind would be sufficient. Since the prophet conveys a noncognitive message, a receptive heart is indispensable. Finally we discover that the prophet points to the unity of the spheres through his unity of speech. The oneness of relationship which overcomes the plurality of experience is, for Buber, the message underlying the prophetic utterance. Buber called art a "witness of the relation" between men and substance; "it is the realm of 'the between' which has become a form."[27] Prophetic artistry is also a witness, a witness to the possibility of relationship through man's response to the divine. Prophetic address is a call to recognize the possible unity of life, the potential relationship hidden in all aspects of human existence.

Buber explains that the Hebrew word for prophet, "nabi," is an indication of the call to relationship. The Hebrew root from which the noun comes means "to speak out," or "to set forth." Buber sees the prophetic task as that of speaking out, of setting forth the opportunity for relationship in the historical context. "To be a Nabi," Buber comments, "means to set the audience, to whom the words are addressed, before the choice and decision, directly or indirectly."[28] What Spinoza sees as "imagination" is for Buber a pedagogical use of historical stimuli; the prophetic imagination uses historical images to evoke human responsiveness:

> The pure prophet is not imaginative or, more precisely, he has no other imagination than the full grasping of the present, actual and potential. His God is the God of a truth which, as far as it is open to mortal man, enters really into time, interwoven with human deeds and misdeeds, that is, it can never be depicted before hand.[29]

Buber insists that the prophet is not imaginative in a Spinozistic sense. The prophetic vision may not increase our knowledge or information but it is not an empty or trivial artistic expression. Prophetic language points to a realm of truth, science, or imagination. Spinoza's rigid dichotomy between rational truth and irrational imagination ignores a third sphere—that of encounter. In that sphere imagination is not deceptive, it serves truth and is no longer make-believe, pretense, a lie. Imagination is a lie only if it sets itself up as truth. The prophet uses imagination to prepare people to make decisions: "The true prophet does not announce an immutable decree. He speaks into the power of decision lying in the moment."[30] Imagination is useful because it stimulates people to think, to become aware, to take risks. To read the prophets correctly one must be responsive to that power of decision lying in one's own moment as well as to that present for the audience to whom the prophet addressed himself. What is new in prophecy is that the prophet enters into a relationship with his audience; not merely his words but his person places the demand for decision upon them. To scientific truth and imaginative fancy the prophet adds a third reality: the truth of encounter.

Not only prophecy, but the Bible as a whole seems to Buber to be a text pointing to relationship and decision-making. The biblical corpus, he claims, "is really one book, for one basic theme unites all the stories and songs, sayings and prophecies contained within it."[31] The theme referred to is that of encounter, and to the reader unprepared to acknowledge the reality of relationship, the Bible is a sealed book.

A reader like Spinoza inevitably misunderstands the Bible since he misses its central reality. The Bible is important not as much for its finalized form as for the germ of relationship from which it sprang. To discover that original seed, however, the reader must be prepared to engage himself with the text in a novel way. Buber holds that to comprehend the Bible one must "forsake the pale of literature for that singular region where great personal religious experiences are propagated."[32] The historical language of the Bible masks its universal meaning.

Although biblical words are couched in specific historical terms, their meaning goes out to all historical periods. All readers are addressed by the biblical message "as directly as if they were hearers, to recognize their situation's demand and to act accordingly."[33]

The modern reader of the Bible is thus directly addressed by its invitation to encounter. Modern man can feel the greatness of the Bible if he views the book not as a history text but as a living voice. That voice issues from the events described and "wishes to communicate to him, its witness, to his constitution, to his life, to his sense of duty."[34] The reader who takes the Bible seriously cannot escape its demand; the Bible testifies that human life has a depth dimension, that choice is possible, that there is more to being human than merely following the changing tides of fate.

This message and demand is precisely the one to which *I and Thou* bears witness. Buber reads the Bible as literature born out of and bearing testimony to the realm of I-Thou being. The Bible is essential for the modern Jew because it stands as a guidepost pointing beyond the trap of I-It life to the freedom of I-Thou. Biblical literature is thus a cornerstone of modern Judaism. Not all of Jewish literature, however, is as clearly relational as the Bible. Even the Bible gives evidence of nonrelational elements in Hebraic religion. While muted in biblical texts such elements are often predominant in later Jewish literature.

Rabbinic Judaism and Buber

One literature which appeared intractable to Buber's mode of interpretation was that created by the early rabbis. These shapers of early Judaism from about 30 B.C.E. to 500 C.E. surrounded Jewish life with a hedge of legalistic writings and spiced it with delightful anecdotes, folktales, and lyrical stories and fables. The former literature is called "halachah" or "the way." As a means of protecting the Jew in exile from the myriad temptations along his path, the rabbinic leaders erected a highway of law, walled in on either side. This law became the means by which the Jew learned what was holy and what was profane, how everyday acts fell into a pattern of religious life, and what God expected of every individual. This halachah, this way of living, provided a common religiousness for all Jews. It left little room for individual differences or innovation.

The second type of literature written by these early rabbis preserves a spirit of individualism, innovation, and fantasy. Into the "aggada," or "tales" as they are called, rabbinic Judaism channeled the imaginative and creative impulses of the Jewish people. Here too, however, a stereotyped literature emerged in which symbols, saints, and rituals received a fixed form.

Buber was ambivalent to rabbinic Judaism. He noted that the very elements which are concentrated in Hasidism "are to be found in a less condensed form everywhere in Judaism, even in 'rabbinic' Judaism." Perhaps he was uneasy with the role of the rabbi through whom the religious life of the individual was processed. No spontaneous, immediate religious response was possible in rabbinic Judaism because of the strict guidelines and forms the rabbis established. The rabbis were disciples of Moses, who stood between God and the people, whereas Buber saw himself as a disciple of Abraham, an example of personal religiousness.[35] More than the roles of rabbinic Judaism, however, it was its literature that caused Buber the greatest concern.

Rabbinic literature presents a peculiar problem for Buber. Its style is legalistic; laws, authorities, closely argued details of practice, constitute its content. In frustration, Buber speaks of the need to "extricate the unique character of Jewish religiosity from the rubble with which rabbinism and rationalism have covered it."[36] Far from representing Jewish religiosity, the ancient rabbis seem to have obscured the truth of Jewish religion. "For untold generations," Buber lamented, "the Jews observed the six hundred and thirteen injunctions of the Torah; but the charge which is higher than every formulation of individual precepts was not fulfilled."[37] The rabbis had set up a barrier of law between religion and religiosity.

On the other hand, Buber responded to the non-legalistic elements in rabbinic lore. Stories about saints and fables about the Jewish past fascinated him. This "aggada," or folklore, was traditionally seen as less important than the legalistic or "halachic" aspects of Judaism. Buber saw it as expressing the underground current of true religiosity which pulsated through Jewish religion even in rabbinic times. Embedded in the aggada Buber found "the development of the people's spirit." But this spirit was repressed by official leaders. The aggada might have altered the atmosphere of rabbinic Judaism but failed; it "did not succeed because its influence had been only fragmentary."[38]

Rabbinic Judaism provides Buber with an example of a Judaism that did not work. A Judaism divided against itself, inevitably split between elite and popular religion, could not transform individuals or be transformed by them. A community pulled apart by polar tensions and not united by a common center was doomed for disaster. Buber's vision was of an integration of religiosity and formal religion. Guideposts from the past might point to the fulfillment of this ideal, to its realization in the present. But by its very nature rabbinic Judaism seems to contradict Buber's insistence on a whole, integrated human life, a life searching for unity.

Buber's approach to rabbinic Judaism gives us a clue to his own thought because his interpretation is a personal one not shared by all scholars. Buber's preconceptions become clear when we compare his work on rabbinic Judaism with that of another Judaic scholar—Leo Baeck. Baeck was roughly contemporary with Buber, living from 1873–1956; and like Buber he wrote on biblical themes, rabbinic Judaism, and theological studies.[39] Unlike Buber, however, Baeck pointed to the polarities in rabbinic Judaism as the basis of Judaism's positive approach to life. Both Baeck and Buber admit the duality of mysticism and legalism in rabbinic Judaism. Buber, however, makes a point of the tension and strain between the two and speaks of "the struggles between the natural structure of a mythical-monotheistic folk-religion and the intellectual structure of a rational-monotheistic rabbinic religion."[40] Baeck contends in contrast that the legalistic and mystical elements, the intellectual structure and the folk-culture, are united in a total unity. A history of Jewish folk-religion and rabbinic religion would, he claims, "be the same history. And for the most part it would be the history of the same men."[41] Where Buber sees tension, strife, disunity, and struggle, Baeck sees harmony, interdependency, and complementary activities.

Even with reference to the same texts the two theologians come to drastically divergent, even contradictory, conclusions. A well-known rabbinic maxim asserts that this world is but an antechamber for the world to come. The text attributed to Rabbi Yaakov goes on to state that: "Better is one hour of *teshuvah* and good deeds in this world than all the life of the world to come. And better is one hour of spiritual refreshment in the world to come than all the life of this world" (Talmud Tractate Avot 4:17).

The most obvious questions to put to this text are the meaning of "better" (Hebrew: *yafa*), the implication of *teshuvah,* and the difference between "life" in the world to come and "spiritual refreshment" in the world to come. These issues, however, are left undiscussed by both Baeck and Buber. Buber finds himself responding to the elevation of *teshuvah* (usually translated as "repentance," but perhaps better rendered as "return" to God). He uses the text to indicate that "The great decision is the supreme moment in the life of man, indeed in the life of the entire world." He goes on to explain why "the life of the world to come," that is to say noncorporeal, completely spiritual life after death, life in which decision-making as we know it is impossible, is considered less desirable than this world of corporeality, suffering, and torments of decisions. This world is the arena of human troubles and as such has been devaluated by many great religions. The world to come is a projected vision of perfection, of peace, of totality and as such has been exalted by major religious dreamers. Buber justifies the text in its advocacy of this world of temporal sorrows over against the world to come and its future perfection: "For the latter is merely being, whereas the former is the great becoming. Sin means to live not in freedom, that is, decision-making, but in bondage, that is, being acted upon, conditioned. The man who 'returns' rises to freedom; he rises from conditionality into unconditionality."[42] Buber ignores the second part of the quotation and, taken out of context, makes the first part a hidden argument for decision-making. Buber is clearly responding to stimuli that lie below the surface meaning of the text. Surely he cannot claim to be providing a literal exegesis, even in the broad sense he claims with the Bible. Buber quite consciously—it cannot be otherwise—wrenches a text out of its rabbinic framework. His defense for this act of violence is given above. Jewish religiosity is encrusted with rabbinic additions. Such, at least, is Buber's spontaneous answer to the text. Given such a response he cannot help but find the world of rabbinic Judaism hopelessly divided against itself.

Baeck, on the other hand, takes the text at face value—the entire text. He does not deny that the two halves of the statement *seem* to contradict each other (that *seem* is my own; unlike Baeck I find that when each term is correctly defined there is no contradiction), and he glories in this contradiction. "Here again," he notes, "we find that tension between the near and the far—the tension between man's goal and his place . . . between the uncertainty which lies in the mystery and the certainty which is given in the command."[43] He takes the text quoted as characteristic of Judaism's ability to "reconcile" seeming opposites. The wholeness of Jewish religion, its ability to encompass law and response, is summed up here.

Both Buber and Baeck have taken Rabbi Yaakov's statement out of context. Buber uses the text to elaborate his own idea of responsibility; Baeck uses it to illustrate his categories of "classical" and "romantic" religiousness.[44] Such arbitrariness is surprising in both thinkers since they show evidence in other places of being sensitive and responsive to the context in which a text appears. Baeck, for example, investigates the biographies of Rabbi Yose ben Yoezer and Rabbi Yose ben Yohanan, two figures placed at the beginning of the rabbinic chain of tradition found in tractate Avot. In that investigation he insists on the relevance of historical context and personality. The development of the Hasmonean kingdom—geographically, socially, and religiously—

shaped the religious thought of these thinkers. Even Jewish mysticism, Baeck contends, did not arise in a vacuum but reflects the historical situation with its intellectual and religious confusion and diversity. The difference between early mystics and later ones can be understood by reference to history.[45]

Baeck's use of texts to prove a tendentious point can be traced to his polemical concerns. Baeck was an apologete for Judaism and sought to discredit the view that Christianity is superior to Judaism. He used texts like the one cited above to contrast the realism of Judaism with the romanticism of Christianity. His disregard of context and personality was stimulated by his effort to demonstrate the superiority of Jewish thinking to the romantic "faith of Paul."[46]

Unlike Baeck, Buber approached rabbinic literature from the standpoint of what he called the "teaching" of Judaism. Teaching referred not to a set of texts, or even a system of ideas. By "teaching" Buber referred to the model provided by living examples of religiousness.

When the Jewish child is taught the Talmud he is taught to relive ancient debates, to take the part of the ancient rabbis. Sometimes he must imaginatively recreate the argument of a great scholar on the basis of one fragment from a fully developed discussion; at other times he is asked to consider whether one view held by a certain rabbi is consistent with another view attributed to that same rabbi elsewhere. In this way ideas are made less important than personality. In actual practice the study of the Talmud often becomes a dull and boring process of memorizing various "positions" attributable to various rabbis. Buber sought in the Talmud those texts which were irreducible to ideas, that could live only as expressions of individual personalities.

Seeking "teaching" rather than doctrine Buber forced the Talmud to develop rabbinic personalities in more depth and detail than in fact the material warranted. Recognizing this Buber himself soon turned to other sources of Jewish "teaching"; the Hasidic leader was such an example. Yet even in the Talmud Buber insisted there was a strand of meaning intrinsically tied to persons rather than thoughts, words, or rational argument. He discovered a number of texts which served his purpose and he pursued their interpretation. One such text is found in the talmudic tractate *Taanit*. This rabbinic source abounds in legendary biographies, such as that of Honi Ha Meagel, a wonderworking rainmaker, whom Buber sees as a man "devoted to God, whose heart is open to his fellow-men and with a reputation for 'clean hands.' " Buber takes such a figure seriously and allows him the freedom to stand as a full-fledged personality, inviolable even in his extremism. Taanit also exalts the figure of Rabbi Zeira, whose complete devotion to the land of Israel compels him to forget all he has learned before coming there. Buber marvels at his patience, self-disregard, ability to allow others to outwit him, abuse him physically, and remain withal happy in an innocent devotion to God and men.[47] Buber does not hold up such fanatic devotion as a model for emulation, but the truth inherent in such a life makes any attempt to wrench the person from his context unacceptable.

The terse legalistic phrases of most of the talmudic literature—including tractate Avot—place no such constraints on Buber. Here he found disembodied fragments which demanded subjective response rather than open acceptance. Buber felt keenly that rabbinic literature was divided against itself. The *aggada* provided folk-heroes and a realistic impetus to the life of I-Thou. The *halacha* countered with abstract ideals and laws, inspiring and lofty, perhaps, but remote from lived experience. Buber described rabbinic Judaism as torn by a deep bifurcation—the realm of human living and the realm of the mind, the realm of folklore and the realm of law, the realm of religious structure and the realm of lived religiosity were divorced from each other. The synthesis of form and content, or religion and religiosity, that he sought was lacking.

Because of this disjointedness Buber felt impelled to reject rabbinic Judaism as a model for a modern Jewish religiosity. Does this rejection mean that he represents "nonrabbinic Judaism?" Does it mean that the law, given at Sinai, is irrelevant to Jewish religiosity? If that were so Buber would be a representative of "pre-Sinaitic" Judaism and be restricted to the content rather than the form of Jewish life. Too much within Buber speaks against such an interpretation. He himself, as we have seen, insisted that Jewish religiosity was present also in rabbinic Judaism. He refused to dissociate himself from the entire chain of tradition which stretched from Abraham through the modern period.

If rabbinic Judaism is not a model of religiosity—as the biblical accounts preserve—then what does Buber find essential in it? Let us ask again what Buber did with rabbinic literature. He used its pithy sayings to awaken reflections on human existence. He was reminded of heroes who had led the life of teaching. These two aspects of rabbinic texts give them their significance. As part of the great tradition of Jewish religiosity rabbinic Judaism jogs the memory and stimulates creative Jewish thinking. The memory of the Jewish past is a creative force only if it is awakened to growth and development. Buber claimed that rabbinic texts served just that purpose. Addressing the Frankfurt Lehrhaus he asked why the modern Jew should study talmudic texts and replied: "Sons and grandsons have the memory of their fathers and forebears in their bones. But such remembering . . . is jogged by a force that wakens and reveals."[48] Contemplating texts and personalities of rabbinic Judaism is such a force. Buber, however, longed for more than the biblical record of holy events and the force in rabbinic Judaism that jogs the memory. He sought a model of true religiosity, a model he found in Hasidism.

Hasidism as Jewish Teaching

Buber was restless with the academic task of interpreting texts—a religious work should be its own interpretation. Texts concerned with ideas and arguments need interpretations; those depicting human lives speak for themselves. As a hermeneutic *I and Thou* drew attention to these undervalued elements in Judaism. Judaism possessed "teaching"—lives which reveal religious truth—and *I and Thou* cultivated a sensitivity to this deeper level of Jewish truth. Teachings reveal lives in which spiritual freedom and loyalty to institutional structure are reconciled. A human being is both a unique spiritual creator and a delighted heir to a tradition, a community, and a structured way of life. The tension between authority and independent thinking which naturally accompanies any approach to a sacred scripture is overcome when lives rather than texts are central. Buber found the finest example of Jewish teaching in Hasidism. Unlike rabbinic Judaism, Hasidism integrated structure and spirituality, or at least Buber's Hasidism did! This environment of integrated religion and religiosity cultivated the growth of the religious ideal—a life lived in the categories of "teaching." Buber translated this ideal into literary form in his renditions of Hasidic anecdotes. These folk-products were for him representative, and he saw them as a concentrated expression of "Jewish teaching." By this he meant that Hasidism represented more than Jewish dogma, philosophy, or legalism. Hasidism expressed Judaism as a pattern of living. Hasidism, he explained, "was not a teaching which was realized by its adherents in this or that measure, but a way of life."[49] When selecting which of the various Hasidic texts he should utilize Buber had this principle in mind. Those texts which demonstrated the "way of life," rather than those concerning theology, were of paramount importance to him. He ordered the tales in a "biographical" arrangement so that the pattern of life involved could become clear. His object was to present "the best account of the character and way of a certain Zaddik."[50] Naturally his subjective and selective approach did not yield an objective, historically rigorous picture of Hasidism. Scholars of Jewish mysticism have sufficient grounds for their criticism of Buber's Hasidism.[51]

The worth of Buber's reconstruction of Hasidic tales needs to be evaluated in different terms. Walter Kaufmann calls the Hasidic tales "great religious stories," and they need to be looked at from that perspective.[52] Buber's transformation of Hasidism was part of an attempt to revive Jewish religiosity, a religiosity which had been drained of power and effectiveness. By rendering the tales of the Hasidim in new and striking language Buber hoped to overcome the "postulate of the hour—to demythologize religion."[53] In his own eyes Buber saw himself as a new disciple of Hasidism. He was to bring the older tradition into a new world, to revive the "teaching" by addressing its lesson to new lives in a new context. He characterized modern times as "the hour when we are in danger of forgetting for what purpose we are on earth" and added that, "I know of no other teaching that reminds us of this so forcibly."[54] Because he fulfills the disciple's task of transmitting the master's message to future generations, Buber claims that "more adequately than the direct disciples, I received and completed the task."[55]

What was this task to which Buber found himself called? We can discover it by analyzing the ways in which Buber used Hasidism. He retold Hasidic tales in the course of describing "the way of man." He collected anthologies of hasidic anecdotes. These two uses of Hasidism complement one another. In the first approach editorial comment, either implied or directly stated, expands the meaning of Hasidism; it makes the modern implication of the older tradition more explicit. The second approach allows the text to speak for itself. It reveals the religious dynamics of the original story without making any direct correlation with modernity. Buber chooses the essay rather than the novel to demonstrate Hasidism's relevance to modern man—his one narrative work, *For the Sake of Heaven,* is more a loosely connected collection of tales than an integrated novel. A master of narrative, however, could use the juxtaposition of events, character, and personality to make comments that reveal the modern situation in relationship to Hasidism. When we analyze Buber it would be useful to have a "control" text, another version of the same tales against which to measure his variations. While the original texts may be useful when we are concerned with Buber's anthologies, they are less helpful when looking at his essays. We need to look at someone who, like Buber, comments, even obliquely, on the tales he tells. That author need not be an essayist. He can be a narrator who uses the Hasidic tale creatively.

There is a tradition of retelling Hasidic stories stretching in modern Jewish intellectual history from the satirist Joseph Perl in the nineteenth century through Eli Wiesel in contemporary literature. Buber merits comparison with all of these. For our study, however, we will concentrate on his relationship to the master Hasidic narrator of our times—Nobel award winner Samuel Joseph Agnon. Not only were both steeped in Hasidic lore but they even projected a joint editorship of an anthology of Hasidic tales; when that proposal failed to materialize they continued a warm relationship throughout their lives.[56] Agnon dedicated a collection of Hasidic stories to Buber.[57] Buber reciprocated this acknowledgment by commenting during an introduction to a collection of essays on Hasidism: "Right now while writing this introduction I have opened a bundle of folios and fragments from Agnon's hand dating from 1921–1924 and have spread them around me. What an influx of living tradition."[58] Clearly the two writers had much in common.

Just because of their commonality the difference in tone and atmosphere between the two authors' approach to Hasidism is significant. Agnon's irony provides a useful contrast to Buber's lyricism, a contrast that stems more from the fundamental presuppositions of each writer rather than from their respective sources. Often the same story appears in startlingly different guise in each of the writers' works. The way each sketches his characters, fills in details, and directs the progress of the action reveals a specific intention, a particular judgment on Jewish religiousness.

Not only Hasidic stories but Hasidic motifs are handled with striking contrast by Buber and Agnon. Hasidism followed classical Jewish mysticism in linking the supernatural and sublunar worlds; above and below are intricately related. No ordinary event is devoid of supernatural meaning for the Hasid whose hero is the ordinary man whose everyday activities unify the divine presence. For Hasidism this theme implied the unity of the profane and the holy. No thought was too coarse to be lifted up in holiness. Sexual fantasies, material needs, and business affairs are as sacred as prayer, study, and acts of piety. Both Agnon and, as we have seen, Buber make use of this theme and weave it into their respective writings.

Agnon's use of this motif is apparent in *Agunot,* the story from which he took his pen name. The story begins by relating the Hasidic belief that from Israel's deeds emanates a thread of grace with which God binds the world together. This motif comments ironically upon the alienation and disjunctive relationships characterizing the protagonists of the story. Another occurrence of the motif is equally ironic. Raphael, the hero of the *Tale of the Scribe,* binds the quality of morning to the quality of evening; he struggles to bring all of God's attributes into harmony. His own life, however, is pervaded by alienation: he is estranged from his wife, unable to accept modernization, and finally isolated from other human beings.

Perhaps the most powerful use Agnon makes of this motif for ironic purposes occurs in his tale *Ha-Malbush, The Garment.*[59] A tailor sits stitching at the end of day, frantically huddled in his corner attempting to complete a garment for the lord of the manor. Only one thing remains to be done—what that is Agnon does not disclose—to transform the collection of materials into a garment. This mystic completion never occurs as one distraction after another deflects the tailor from his task. These distractions are both holy and profane: pious prayer, washing of the hands, and thoughts of ethics are as distracting as thoughts about liquor, dinner, or displaced anger. Agnon seems to be hinting that while religious idealists seek unity, here below such ideals are out of place. And not only here below. Just as the lord of the manor is just but his servants are cruel, so Agnon explains that the Lord above is merciful but his servants are not. The three stories *Agunot, Agadat Ha-Sofer* (The Tale of the Scribe), and *Ha-Malbush* emphasize how far modern man is from reaching the ideal of unification. Agnon's stories use the theme of unity as an ironic commentary on the conflicted and tortured lives of human beings.

Buber, as has already been made clear by his use of the anecdote "Patchwork" and his exploration of the "two foci of the Jewish soul," exalts the theme of unity. Hasidism sets a goal for the Jew which should in fact be the goal of all men. Buber is particularly fond of the tale of Enoch the cobbler. Enoch sits in his shop (echoes of Agnon's tailor!) and sews together the upper leather and the sole of the shoe. As he does this he joins together God and his Shekina (an ideal which motivated the Scribe, but which only frustrated his involvement in life). Buber finds in Judaism a definite concern with distinguishing between the holy and the profane, between everyday life and sacred tasks. But he also notes an antithetical theme opposing it: the desire to sanctify the everyday. "The wish still awakes ever again," he comments, "to invest the holy with effect and influence in the realm of the profane"; and when Hasidism fashioned the story of Enoch into its own form, "this wish now entered into fulfillment."[60]

At the heart of the difference between Agnon and Buber is the latter's sense of Judaism's dynamic nature. Buber assumes unity to be the goal and Judaism as a process working toward that goal. Agnon assumes Judaism to be a self-sufficient end in itself. As such its expectations of men are unrealistic. Buber agrees that most of us cannot live up to the ideal represented by Enoch. He sympathizes with the conflicted soul. But religion should be a force propelling us to a higher level of existence. Because religion is religiosity—a process of becoming—Buber is not as distraught by the gap between reality and ideal as Agnon.

The distinction between Buber's dynamic approach and Agnon's view of Judaism is evident in the way each uses a tale which stresses the exception rather than the rule in Hasidic behavior. The tale centers on a Hasid who abandons the frenzy of enthusiastic ecstasy for quiet stillness. Both Buber and Agnon begin this narrative by referring to the talmudic precedent of rabbis who moved so uncontrollably during prayer that "if you left him in one corner, when you returned he was in the opposite one." Both continue by noting the Hasid who, in exception to this tradition, remained absolutely still. From Agnon we have this tale in *Agadat Ha-Sofer*. On the ecstatic holiday of Simhat Torah, when all were dancing in wild frenzy, Raphael's chanting created a stillness, a rigid quiet. Symbolically this event points to Raphael's petrified life, his frozen religiousness which finally sacrifices both him and his wife to the ultimate stillness—death.[61]

Buber's tale speaks more positively. It tells of Yehuda Loeb, who remained motionless while the great Zaddik of Lublin prepared to say the benediction on Sukkot. (Is it just a coincidence that Simhat Torah falls on the additional day at the end of Sukkot?) The Zaddik was convulsed by ecstatic motions that sent all other observers reeling and swaying. Yehuda, however, waited patiently for the blessing itself and "looked up at the now motionless, exalted master and heard the divine blessing."[62] The quiet of religion is an attentive listening for Buber, not a symbol of petrification. Inactivity symbolizes rigidity for Agnon; Buber transforms it into an intimation of religious vitality and sensitivity.

Buber's view of Judaism as a dynamic religion leads him to an appreciation of the folk element foreign to Agnon. He recounts that Rabbi Yitzkak of Kalev inherited the melody used by the Great Maggid for chanting the song "Adir Bimlucha" for the Passover Seder and notes that it had been learned from a wandering shepherd. With equal seriousness Buber records that the song itself had been "in exile with the shepherd, for originally the Levites had sung it in the Temple."[63] Passover, of course, is itself a folk festival, and the concluding hymns at the Seder are appropriately folkloristic. In Buber's telling of the anecdote he acknowledges this folk element and then in all seriousness grants it a religious significance equal to that of the Temple cult.

Agnon's short novel *In the Heart of the Seas* is difficult to decipher.[64] The reader hardly knows when Agnon is being ironic or when serious. Yet when he praises Gentiles who have been blessed with the tunes used for a penitential hymn of the Day of Atonement, the reader can be a bit skeptical. Unlike Passover, the Day of Atonement is a spiritual, not a folk, holiday, characterized by solemnity rather than folkloristic humor. The paragraph describing this "gift to the pious gentiles" is preceded by a description of the Jewish cemeteries. This juxtaposition is ironic in itself. The reader is also led to wonder whether the pious narrative may not be a bit propagandistic. If Gentiles are rewarded for their pious fidelity by being granted a Jewish melody, how much more so should Jews having this melody be faithful and pious.

Agnon views faith as simple and naive, so naive that strikingly simple and pietistic beliefs can coexist with the most grotesque, outlandish, and patently ridiculous creations of folklore. He blurs the distinction between pristine religious faith and superstitious imaginings of an ignorant and frightened folk culture. Both images rooted in the Jewish tradition and weird notions borrowed from pagan imagination are equally potent and omnipresent in his stories but the two stand in contrast and contradiction to each other. For Agnon this unseemly blend of the Judaic and the pagan gives the lie to Jewish pietism. Buber does not deny an interrelationship between Jewish and non-Jewish folklore, but he rejoices in this blend. He acknowledges that the song may seem to be foreign, but then he traces its ancestry back to Temple times. Agnon's telling of the tale makes one suspect whether the story of the gentile piety may not be a self-serving justification for cultural borrowing. Agnon does not trace the song back to the Temple—it is a purely Jewish song for Yom Kippur—but relates that the Gentiles have earned the right to it. By keeping his explanation tied to the present Agnon has also made it rather unbelievable.

The use of folk materials in religion is not the only form of creativity. The individual molds new forms as well. Hasidism records such creative activity. Buber, naturally, bases his renewal of Judaism on just such elements in Hasidism. The tendency for innovation enables religiosity to remain alive and vital. A modern Judaism would be responsive to such innovations. Buber notes that sometimes "the soul lays hold of the voice of a man and makes it sing." Spirit, to use the language of *I and Thou,* confronts man and demands fulfillment. Religion is the response to that demand. Hasidic religion, for Buber, recognizes and integrates such religiosity into its inner nature. He cites the Zaddik who on the Day of Atonement sang new melodies, "wonder of wonder, that he had never heard and that no human ear had ever heard."[65] Describing the motivation for such acts Buber remarks on two demands: first, unification "to one true congregation to furnish the site for the union with God; second, that they detach their prayers from individual wishes." Innovation springs, Buber implies, from an abandonment of self. "This was the spirit," Buber comments, "in which . . . he abandoned the charted track of memory and custom and sang new melodies, never heard before."[66] Creativity in religious forms derives from selflessness, from complete concentration on the address from the Eternal Thou. In Buber's retelling, Hasidic stories of innovation become stories of the flexibility of religious forms because Buber's view of religiosity—of artistic creation— roots it in a responsive dedication to a demand coming from the realm of spirit.

Agnon, of course, had no such view of creativity. The artist, and for him particularly the writer, must draw upon his own inner resources. The story *Im Kenisat HaYom*—At the Onset of Dusk—represents the total isolation of the artist. The traditional home offers no refuge to the hero and his daughter who are fleeing after "enemies destroyed my house." Remembered heroes, rabbis, companions, books, are all insufficient. Finally the daughter covers herself with her own hair, envelops herself with herself and repeats the prayers of the Day of Atonement "in sweet melodies unheard by any ear before."[67] The self must create out of itself. The artistic form which Buber saw as emerging from an encounter is for Agnon the product of the isolated self. Buber appropriates the Hasidic story as proof of his religious theory. Agnon uses it to focus on the individual as the creative nucleus.

Throughout this contrast with Agnon, Buber has consistently been the more constructive. The Hasidic story provides a foundation for a renewed Jewish religiousness, a living religiosity. Buber uses the Hasidic anecdote to demonstrate the flexibility and dynamic qualities of a religiousness which is alive, vital, and developmental despite adherence to a formal religious tradition. Agnon's use of the same material focuses on the ironic contradiction inherent in any organized religiousness—the static and frozen elements which render the pretense of vitality ridiculous and implausible. Buber suggests new ways of being religious by contrasting the ideal of unity and the reality of human divisiveness; Agnon finds in that contrast the basic self-contradiction of religion. Buber considers Hasidic folk material proof of a growing vitality of religious institutions; Agnon considers that folklore evidence of the superstitious quality of religious life and uses the Hasidic folktale ironically.

Turning to the folktales themselves, both Buber and Agnon offer anthologies of Hasidic anecdotes. Buber selects stories that exalt persons. Agnon focuses the tales to praise books. Buber looks for sensitivity and human responsiveness; Agnon points out extremism and excess. Examples of these differences could be multiplied; for this investigation four will demonstrate the point. In each tale Agnon can be seen as emphasizing books, extremist religion, and static forms while Buber focuses on human life, evolving religious forms, and responsive religiosity.[68]

The first example concerns the "Or Ha-Ganuz"—the light hidden for the righteous—from which Buber's book takes its Hebrew name. In the front of that book Buber records his version of the story.[69] Buber unfolds his narrative through the use of dialogue. Unnamed students question anonymous respondents (the emphasis on the plural is noteworthy here). Light is hidden for the righteous, the students admit, but where can it be found? In the Torah, comes the reply. But then wouldn't the Zaddikim have found it? They have done so? But then where is it revealed? In their lives. The key word in Buber's telling of the tale is "finding." The light can be found by the Zaddikim and found in the lives of the Zaddikim. Religious living is a process of discovery and of communication. The two are interwoven—to discover the light in literature means to reveal it in life. Light is a transparent metaphor for religious vitality; finding emphasizes that such vitality is not static but constantly renewed.

Agnon tells the same story as a miracle tale.[70] Whenever the Baal Shem Tov (note the singularity here) would meet someone who demanded help—locating a lost relative, discovering a misplaced article, or the like—he would study a holy text. The disciples were curious—could answers to such mundane issues be found in those sources? The Besht answered that from the light hidden in these books he could see "from one end of the world to the other" and thus discover that which his petitioner was missing. In Agnon's version the idea of "discovery" is taken in literal terms. Such discovery is mundane and very much a "miracle." It is also static; religious practice lacks the dynamic concern for lives and religiosity which Buber makes paramount. Buber's spiritual rendition makes Agnon's tale seem like a reduction of Hasidism to magic.

Even when Buber allows books to have a power all their own, it is far from a magical one. One tale that exemplifies this approach is "The Book."[71] The story is narrated in the first person by one who as a young child had been brought by his father to see Rabbi Yaakov Yosef, author of the *Toldoth,* a collection of the Besht's teachings. The innocent wonder of youth pervades the tale and gives it a charming simplicity. The boy relates that his father continually studied Rabbi Yaakov Yosef's work and pondered its meaning. Once he found a particular passage puzzling. Taking up his son he harnessed the horses and rode away to see the sage. Yaakov Yosef, on his deathbed, was courteous to his visitors. When told the reason for their visit, he seizes the book and explains the passage in a strong, enthusiastic voice. The boy relates in amazement, "it seemed to me that the bed was lifted high above the earth." Buber finds in this story, one can deduce, an example of the close unity between book and author, creator and his creation. The artistic work gives renewed strength to its originator. A book is more than mere words, it is also testimony to a vital life-force.

Agnon's version of the tale is freighted with ritualism and pietistic formula.[72] The narrative begins with a panegyric in praise of Rabbi Moses and his excessive love for the book *Toldot.* The haste of his visit to Rabbi Yaakov Yosef is conveyed not by mundane images—Buber's harnessing of the horses—but by saying "he took his talit and tefillin." Ritualism rather than realism provides the central focus. At the same time, the naive wonder of the child is transformed into grotesque realism. The bed of which Buber wrote—"it seemed lifted high above the earth"—is described by Agnon as literally hanging from the rafters. When Rabbi Yaakov Yosef becomes filled with holy fervor the bed swings like a pendulum causing the walls to quake. The old rabbi who has just been compared to a one-year-old babe produces a veritable earthquake! From what does this new strength derive? Not from the dynamic influx of creative artistry but from name magic. When pronouncing the name of the Besht the rabbi renews his fervor. The climax of the story comes when Yaakov Yosef points to the stars and announces: "These stars look small to us, but in truth each star is a world itself; so it is with every word of my master."

Here as previously, Agnon's view of religion emphasizes the static while Buber's is more dynamic. Agnon restricts religious power to that which is supernatural. As we have seen before Buber relegates the miraculous to the realm of subjective response. It occurs within a human being. Agnon's view is more conventional—a miracle is a wondrous event in external reality. Buber's narrative appears more direct and simple than Agnon's. The latter has an eerie, gothic, almost humorous, quality. Buber integrates Hasidic wonders and natural life; Agnon presents them as mysteriously supernatural.

Perhaps Agnon gives this impression because he sees Jewish leadership as dependent upon supernatural claims and autocratic procedures. He roots authority in the sense of dependency cultivated in the common Jew. Buber claims that Hasidic leadership emerged naturally from an organic communal life. Agnon sees the community as the audience and the Zaddik as the wonder-working central actor. This difference between Buber and Agnon becomes clear in a story which Buber calls "Sound of the Great Trumpet."[73] The Baal Shem Tov, according to this tale, lived some distance from his companions. After he had delivered a lesson on the text "Sound the trumpet for our freedom," the companions went to their retreat in the woods while the master retired to his chambers. The narrator of the tale remained behind in the house of the Besht since "I never thought to go with them or unite with them since I was still young." Suddenly he felt an overwhelming intuition that the Messiah was coming. Would he meet no welcoming group of Jews? In order to rectify this situation the narrator began to run toward the companions in the woods. He finds them seated at a table without the power of speech. He unites himself with their silence and when the messianic expectation passes they remain together.

Once again Agnon tells the story in the third person rather than in the first person.[74] He omits the last detail of the joining of the companions. The hero in Agnon's telling runs to the comrades because he can find no other way of relieving the anxiety of his spirit. His previous reluctance is attributed to his fear that "I dared not go there since I was but a *yanik*." The last term means, literally, an infant, but also brings associations of the "yenuka," or precocious child, found in the *Zohar*. This child has greater insight and scholarly acumen than his elders. Perhaps the narrator is giving evidence of a hidden pride or at least a temptation to demonstrate greater religious perception than his teachers. In any case Agnon's narrator is more self-centered than Buber's and is less oriented toward community.

Even more striking than this example is one in which the Zaddik himself is the central figure. In this tale both Buber and Agnon agree that the great Rebbe Simha Bunam was once tempted to tell a secular joke.[75] Both writers tell how Satan attempted to dissuade the Zaddik by arguing that a secular, profane anecdote is unworthy of his status and position. In each case Rabbi Bunam replies in Aramaic that Satan should not be heeded since he does not understand the deep secrets of Judaism. One such secret is that all joy—even secular jokes—have their origin in the Garden of Eden. The rabbi proceeds to tell the joke. Buber then explains that Rabbi Bunam's leadership grew in existential power. Those who had been far removed from him were joined together with his followers. He unified the community and led many to the true knowledge of God by his act. The story had worked an inner transformation on its auditors.

Agnon's response is more matter-of-fact. Rabbi Bunam began receiving more petitions than he had before. His sphere of authority had broadened. He became the "saint" over a larger population. His reputation as a wonder-working, miraculous figure had been enhanced. For Agnon, the rebbe draws his power from status, the insignia of office, and superstitious belief.

Agnon and Buber approach Hasidism differently because each finds in it a different type of religiousness. This difference is close to that which Henri Bergson characterizes as that between static and dynamic religiousness. The former provides us with support; the latter pushes boundaries aside and opens new vistas to life:

> just as when an artist of genius has produced a work which is beyond us, the spirit of which we cannot grasp, but which makes us feel how commonplace were the things we used to admire, in the same way static religion, though it may still be there is no longer what it was, above all it no longer dares to assert itself.[76]

Buber sees in Hasidism dynamic religion, a religion that awakens new responsiveness and growth. Agnon relegates Hasidism to the realm of the static; it shares with all Jewish religion of the past a frozen, static quality. Buber finds in Hasidism a rejection of that book-centered, ritualistic, life-stultifying traditionalism which Agnon finds that it exemplifies.

This contrast brings into relief two ways in which Judaism may be defined—either classically by its concern for law, authority figures, and books, or imaginatively by its responsive questioning of people, its awakening of instincts, its concern for individuals. Buber's retelling of Hasidism, even if not historically accurate, evokes an imaginative Judaism. With that alternative impressed on the mind it is difficult to accept the classical definition of Judaism as exclusive and self-authenticating. Buber has made the Hasidic hero into a model of teaching. The literary form of Buber's stories is more than literary convention—it attempts to present lively and vital religious models. Agnon's heros are not religious models. They are, perhaps, religious warnings. Buber's heroes entice the reader to follow and promise a religious vitality beyond the experience of any one period in Jewish history. Hasidism is transformed into teaching by Buber's method which restructures older narratives to create a Judaism which is responsive and changing, which is based on persons. It is a Judaism in which dynamic personality dominates and in which the human life rather than the book is central. In many ways the relationship between Agnon and Buber was ironic; one cannot escape the suspicion that Agnon saw this irony. The two authors stood for antithetical reconstructions of Hasidism; they were unalterably opposed in their view of the relevance of Hasidism for modern man. Bergson saw static and dynamic religion as inextricably intertwined although diametrically opposed to each other. "Thus do we find interposed," he suggests, "transitions and differences . . . between two things which are as a matter of fact radically different in nature and which, at first sight, we can hardly believe deserve the same name."[77] The same is true of Agnon and Buber. Hasidism included within itself both static and dynamic elements. Agnon chose to emphasize one side of the Hasidic tale, Buber the other. By contrasting one with the other we have discovered how very different they are. Despite similarities, Agnon's Hasidic tale and Buber's are two radically different phenomena and need to be distinguished from one another. This essay has been a step in that direction.

More importantly, however, this essay has established Buber as a new disciple of Hasidic masters. He was to transform their message by revealing it as teaching. To do this he remolded his material so that dynamic religiousness was revealed. He selected and edited his tales so that the ritualistic and static elements could be disregarded. Buber's task was nothing less than changing a Jew's perception of his religion. Through Hasidism Jewish religion became, in Buber's rendering, a teaching rather than a set of laws and dogmas. Of course Buber wrestled with his texts and recreated their form and style. The contrast with Agnon, however, shows how well he succeeded in his aim, how completely he effected the transformation of Hasidism into a living, dynamic religiosity.

Unlike Agnon, Buber has used Hasidism constructively and creatively. Such use is the crucial distinction between Buber's exegesis and that of other modern writers in general. His biblical writings apply this creativity to a text which scholars treat as dead documentation of past civilization. His fragmented approach to rabbinic literature is nevertheless a successful rejection of the techniques of those who like Leo Baeck build up an esoteric philosophy on the basis of collated talmudic citations. Behind each of these exegetical stances lies the theology of *I and Thou*. Literature is a portal to relationship. Whether the portal becomes a present gate of entrance because it reveals living spirit, exemplary lives, or a dynamic religiosity depends upon the text considered. Buber's major contribution is neither his insight into a text's original meaning nor his reconstruction of the religious reality behind a text. It lies in his ability to transform a relic from the past into a contemporary statement of religious potential. *I and Thou* provides the programmatic foundation; Buber's Jewish exegesis is an extension and application of that program.

I and Thou provides Buber with a means of making a text relevant to contemporary man. Jewish existence, however, depends on more than just texts. Judaism is comprised of directives to action. Buber's emphasis on deed is present in *I and Thou*. How that emphasis reflects and confronts the basic problem of Jewish religious living needs further exploration. Can Buber breathe contemporary life into traditional Jewish practice as he did into classical Jewish texts? This question will provide the focus of our second chapter.

Chapter II

I and Thou and Jewish Ritual

I and Thou *and Ritualism*

Martin Buber has often been criticized because of his restlessness with Jewish law. His philosophy in general and *I and Thou* in particular have been seen as inimical to ritual practice. His views have been interpreted either as outright rejection of ritualism or as suspicious of institutionalized forms.[1] A closer look at *I and Thou,* however, should convince us that ritualism is not condemned out of hand. There are nuances and variations in Buber's approach that need exploration. In order to explore these nuances we can divide our investigation into two parts. The first section will consider Buber's positive view of ritual in general and Jewish ritual in particular. That section will rely most heavily on the specific parts of *I and Thou* which concern ritualism. The second section, however, will raise the question: Why, if his view is positive, does Buber refuse to accept Jewish law as authoritative? No one can deny that in his own life-style and in his response to Franz Rosenzweig Buber appears antinomian, opposed to the very idea of legalism. Law is so central to Judaism that failure to account for it would cast suspicion on Buber's credentials. A Jew cannot fail to confront the idea of *halacha,* of the law. A correct understanding of Buber on this point is thus absolutely crucial.

In *I and Thou* Buber shows that human beings can enter into relationship not only by interhuman encounter but by encounter with nature and spirit. Ritual constructs portals for such encounter. Before discussing how such portals are built it is necessary to review the three spheres of encounter themselves. Buber contends that:

> Three are the spheres in which the world of relation is built. . . .
> In every sphere, in every relational act, through everything that becomes present to us, we gaze toward the train of the eternal You; in each we perceive a breath of it; in every You we address the eternal You, in every sphere according to its manner.[2]

To say that ritual serves as a response to an encounter with the Eternal Thou or provides a foundation for such an encounter is too general. How ritual is effective in each of the three spheres still needs to be explored. The three strands that can be discovered in Buber's theology of Jewish ritual are his view of ritual as a product of the human spirit and thus a partner in post-threshold encounter, his insistence upon the sociological significance of ritual as creative of community and preliminary to a threshold encounter, and his interpretation of certain rituals as a means of enabling an unmediated meeting with nature, as preparation for a pre-threshold encounter.

Ritual and Post-Threshold Encounters

Buber has claimed that one of the achievements of vital religiosity is to "fill vibrant time with new hymns and songs," and such creations are examples of what he calls elsewhere "beings of the spirit." In its most responsive form the "word" spoken or sung is ever and again the occasion for a renewed relationship with the Eternal Thou:

> The word is present in revelation, at work in the life of the form, and becomes valid in the dominion of the dead form.[3]

The primary example of such a ritualism is prophetic preaching. Buber admits that priests as well are entrusted with the word, but for the priest the word is set and administered whereas for the prophet it is always new and surprising: "The rite is a work of man and it is accepted or rejected by God, according to the feelings of the men performing it; whereas the word comes again and again from heaven as something new, and makes its abode within man."[4] As a partner in an encounter the word must be granted its independent existence; it must be permitted freshness and the ability to surprise. Priestly religion—and *halacha* falls into this category—prevents this very freshness. In just such a conflict between surprise and predictability Buber favors the freshness of the prophet. He says with Jeremiah in opposition to the Deuteronomic reformation that the book "which claims to stand good forever, to continue its existence without addition or subtraction," cannot survive alone; "without the rousing and renovating life of the word, even the book does not live."[5] In this recognition of the danger of the fossilization of the living word we find both the uneasiness with a fixed, halachic code and the demand that ritual be responsive and a channel for religiosity which have characterized the way scholars have looked at Buber's view of ritual.

Ritual and Threshold Encounter

Yet for Buber ritual does not need to be seen merely as the vibrant partner in a post-threshold encounter. It can, as easily, be a precondition for other encounters which equally reveal the divine. In this case a more crystallized, legalistic ritual is possible. This ritual, of course, must still be open and free, but its freedom consists in what it points to beyond itself rather than in the active responsiveness to the creative Thou it represents. The sociological value of the Sabbath is a case in point. Buber recognizes the religious validity of Sabbath law. He sees its regulations and definite religious form as positive rather than negative features. The central religious value of the Sabbath, however, is not its

70

ritual power *per se,* but the fact that it establishes a human community which is responsive to the divine.

> We have no clear idea of the Mosaic celebration of the Sabbath, but this is obvious; here again a great step had been taken towards unifying the people, towards bringing the national community into being; and once again, by means of an institution which served to gather Israel around their God.[6]

It is, perhaps, the specific genius of Judaism to conceive of encounter in such a social and communal way. Buber makes the claim that Jewish social legislation has as its goal not merely societal reform but rather religious and ritual implications. Only as a community of interrelating persons can the Israelites truly encounter God:

> The "social" element in the apodictic laws is to be understood not on the basis of the task of bettering the living conditions of society, but on the basis of establishing a true people, . . . the aim of such commands is not the single person, but the "people of YHVH," this people which shall rise, but cannot rise so long as the social distance loosens the connections of the members of the people and decomposes their direct contact with one another.[7]

Thus a second function of ritual for Buber is that of constituting community. Again, as with the first function, this sociological task can become fossilized and stagnant. Whereas creative ritual could become too rigid, sociological ritual can become an end in itself rather than a means to community. Buber's view of community can accept Jewish legalism when it is the expression of a vital communal bond but must reject such legalism when it prevents rather than enables social interaction:

> To be sure, to manifest itself in a community of men, to establish and maintain a community, indeed to exist as a religion, religiosity needs forms; for a continuous religious community, perpetuated from generation to generation is possible only where a common way of life is maintained. But when instead of uniting them for

71

freedom in God, religion keeps men tied to an immutable law and
damns their demand for freedom . . . it transforms the law into a
heap of petty formulas and allows man's decision for right or wrong
action to degenerate into hairsplitting casuistry—then religion no
longer shapes but enslaves religiosity.[8]

In this strand of his approach not creativity as such but
responsiveness to *human dignity* and the true needs of social
existence are the marks of valid ritualism.

Ritual and Pre-threshold Encounters

An encounter can occur not only with spiritual creations or
other human beings but with natural entities as well. Although
this contention of Buber's has often been a perplexing one, it is
nonetheless clear that it is central to his thought. Human beings
can have unmediated relationships with the natural world. Such a
view must be distinguished from pantheistic worship of nature.
Buber insists that "God may be seen seminally within all things,
but He must be realized between them."[9] One of the most
important aspects of ritual for Buber is its ability to transform an
entity of nature into a real and present "other" with whom a
relationship is possible. Ritual can bring the individual into
confrontation with natural entities as true selves, as independent
realities. Judaism provides striking examples of such rituals. The
ritual of the Sabbatical year is seen by Buber as more than a
negative condition: "It is the state of being taken up into the
natural operation of the covenant." It provides land with an
identity and reality of its own when it is "not to be subjected to
the will of man, but left to its own nature."[10] Another such ritual
is that of the offering of the first fruits. Through interaction with
the fruits of the land the individual finds in creation a witness to
God's covenant.[11]

To relate fully and openly with nature there must be a
concrete and actual encounter with the natural world. This third
strand in Buber's thinking emphasizes not so much the creativity
of ritual or its sociological structure as its making bodily and

concrete a spiritual content. Here the ritual act itself is central. Without a personal engagement in the ritual process symbolism is impossible: "No symbol has authentic existence in the spirit if it has no authentic existence in the body."[12] The very definition of ritual as sacrament implies this concrete reality: "a sacrament is the binding of meaning to the body, fulfillment of binding, of becoming bound."[13] In this case ritual is the necessary foundation for genuine character. When Solomon, for example, centralized worship and converted Judaism from being ritually concerned with the soil and the land into a religion of faith in Jerusalem, then Solomon "threatens to hide the appearance of the leader-God himself."[14]

As a means of preserving the human tie with concrete natural reality, the halachic structure is indispensable. Such a personalist ritualism that makes the individual responsible and responsive in his relationships with natural entities preserves the possibility of pre-threshold encounter. Buber's concern is not with flexibility or social accountability of ritual but with its concrete realization of nature as an authentic other. *Halacha* is not merely acceptable but positively imperative to preserve this possibility.

Buber's Antinomianism

Despite these positive aspects deducible from *I and Thou,* Buber's image as an antinomian remains. His bias against Jewish law as expressed in his exchange of letters with Franz Rosenzweig is undeniable. How can he refute Rosenzweig's claim that the law can always be made into a vehicle for relationship? Isn't that just what Buber himself implies? How can he answer Rosenzweig's challenge that he accept the law as openly as he accepts teaching? Rosenzweig grants Buber that Orthodoxy is restricting. He does not deny that the law as interpreted by Samson Raphael Hirsch is an obstacle to encounter. But why should Hirsch have the last word? "Nobody," Rosenzweig contends, "should be allowed to tell us what belongs to its (the law's) spheres."[15]

Is there something, even in *I and Thou* itself, which makes the law different from ritual? Is Buber's bias merely a personal idiosyncrasy or is it rooted in his basic thought? One might think that Buber is antinomian for private reasons. Buber's refusal to acknowledge the possibility of transforming Jewish law into vital religiousness might be attributed to his own biography. His early experiences at home, his parents' divorce, his life with his grandfather might serve as explanations for his rigidity here. His private desire to live free from the shackles of German-Jewish Orthodoxy might explain his rejection of Rosenzweig's proposal. Certainly it seems that his renowned ability to listen openly to others apparently fails him here. He reiterates that the law does not address him personally, that God is never a law-giver although man is of necessity a law-receiver. The analogy which Rosenzweig suggested between openness to the teachings and openness to the law does not exist. The teachings when taken seriously lead directly to decision-making, to God's unconditional demand for spontaneous response. The law, on the other hand, cannot help but obstruct spontaneity; it is by definition incompatible with hearing God's word. What is this except a deliberate deafness to Rosenzweig's proposal? Buber declares that "the division between revelation and teaching (human teaching) is for me neither a thorn nor a trial, but that between revelation and law (human law) is both." The subjective strength of that "for me" lends credence to the argument that Buber's antinomianism is a personal, biographically related quirk unrelated to his general philosophy. Is he not arbitrarily deciding that the law is antithetical to responsiveness? He cries, "I cannot admit the law transformed by men into the realm of my will if I am to hold myself ready as well for the unmediated word of God." Yet such a remark seems to show an almost intentional disregard for Rosenzweig's argument that "the law can be changed back into a commandment."[16] Is this failure of understanding by Buber merely the result of his private history; is it unsupported by his theoretical investigations of Judaism? Certainly the fact that he did not follow more of the commandments, that he personally held aloof from Jewish observance, is an important biographical datum about Buber. But his claim here is not about the observance of this or that ritual. It concerns the very *concept* of law. Buber is making a theological judgment. While his private life may well be grist for the biographer's mill, his attitude toward the concept of law is more appropriately studied in terms of his religious ideas. Rather than assume an arbitrariness in Buber's response to Rosenzweig, let us look at his entire understanding of Judaism and seek a consistency of view that will explain that response.

While Buber's antinomianism cannot, as we have seen, be traced to the view of ritual and cult found in *I and Thou,* it may in fact have its roots somewhere in that book. Buber's restlessness with the legal system may be related to his view of the religious process in general and the Jewish religious process particularly. *I and Thou* posits a basic dichotomy of being—a division that Judaism both exemplifies and at its best tries to transcend. By definition, then, Judaism holds the two poles of spontaneity and legalism in tension. As a religious process it demonstrates both the stage of responsive creativity and of frozen formalism. On the one hand Jewish ritual presents an opportunity for a concrete encounter between the human and the divine. Through it men become aware that nature, other human beings, and spiritual ideals all have a reality of their own. On the other hand ritual, of necessity, becomes institutionalized. It stands as a self-sufficient substitute for relationship. The realm of organizations, of rigid standards, and of formal ritualism must be taken on its own terms. To confuse the stage of legalism with that of responsiveness seems, to him, to be illegitimate, to be untrue to Jewish religiousness.

This approach does not deny the importance of law and institutions. A careful reading of *I and Thou* shows Buber's acknowledgment of the human need for institutions. Laws, rules, sets of obligations and responsibilities are necessary to provide human life with a framework. In order to sanctify daily life men must have guidelines and criteria of holiness. Rules and obligations offer men just such guidance. As definitions of sanctity they prepare the way for spontaneous creation; new spheres of reality are lifted up into holiness and thereby the definition itself is expanded. Through law men distinguish between the holy response and a demonic one. Buber finds in the revelation at Sinai just such a framework for responsible decision-making:

> For the giving of the law at Sinai is properly understood as the body of rules which the divine ruler conferred upon His people in the hour of His ascension to the throne. All the prescriptions of this body of rules, both the ritual and the ethical, are intended to lead beyond themselves into the sphere of the "holy."[17]

If Buber's antinomianism is attributable neither to an intrinsic hostility to ritual nor rules, it is even less related to a denial of the centrality of the law to Jewish religiousness. While distinguishing between Jewish law and the "soul" of Judaism, he nevertheless finds the two intimately tied together. "The Law," he acknowledges, "put on the soul and the soul can never again be understood outside of the Law."[18] While refusing to accept the binding power of the law, Buber does recognize its authority as an expression of the Jewish spirit. Without the law, Buber suggests, Judaism might have become so spiritualized that it would have lost its hold on concrete reality. The Jewish legal spirit derives from that same desire to have the abstract and historically specific elements within life meet—thus was Jewish ritual produced. The law demanding the offering of the first fruits of the land is, for Buber, a protection against the separation of religion and economic life. By its authoritative influence on agricultural life, the cult insured the penetration of the economic sphere by spiritual values. The idea of expressing gratitude to the Creator cannot be abandoned to abstract idealism:

> One must not completely spiritualize such a conception and deprive it of the bodily substance without which the spiritual content would have no real stability. No symbol has authentic existence in the spirit if it has no authentic existence in the body. In order that Israel

may become the first fruits of the divine harvest, it needs a real land as well as a real people.[19]

The law was for Buber a valid formulation of what he called the "deed-tendency." By this he meant the desire to express religiousness through concrete deeds rather than primarily in abstract philosophy or subjective faith. He found it highly ironic that in the wake of the Enlightenment this same battle broke out in the squabbles between the Reform and Orthodox parties of Judaism. Orthodoxy, despite what Buber considered its "ossification" of the law, attempted to defend the deed-tendency in Judaism against the completely spiritualized, abstract, and therefore for Buber, sterile faith enunciated by the Reformers. Even the "bickering, devoid of ideas and spirit, between the Orthodox and Reformers" is considered a worthy example of the Jewish insistence on the primacy of deeds.[20]

Buber's defense of Orthodoxy, and what Franz Rosenzweig rightly sees as his reliance on Samson Raphael Hirsch, needs to be understood in terms of the deed-tendency in Judaism. Buber, like Hirsch before him, saw in the interpretation of Judaism offered first by Baruch Spinoza and then by Moses Mendelssohn the gravest danger facing modern Judaism.[21] Spinoza had claimed that Judaism represented the civil law of the Jewish commonwealth. Mendelssohn modified this view by saying that Judaism was the divine legislation which enable Jews to become good citizens of whatever land they inhabited. Neo-Orthodoxy responded to the utilitarian and civil arguments advanced by Spinoza and Mendelssohn. While not denying the usefulness of the Jewish law code, Hirsch contended that its authority was rooted in its being the content of revelation. Only when God's presence is identified with the law does it have religious significance. Buber sympathizes with this view. He too finds the utilitarianism of Mendelssohn and Spinoza uncongenial. If the law is to have any significance it must be as God's revelation. Buber notes with approval Hirsch's "genuine affirmation of the law" which he finds "anchored in this certitude of the fact of revelation and that its content has been faithfully preserved in the 613 *mitzvoth* and their framework."²² Hirsch rightly sees the law not as authority but as divinely instituted deed. Buber disagrees with Hirsch, claiming that no deed can be premeditated. A deed for Buber must of necessity be spontaneous. Yet if the law is to have religious merit as *content* then it can do so only on the grounds which Hirsch argues. In this positive approach to traditionalism Buber's reluctance to accept Rosenzweig's view of the law is made more plausible: traditionally the law has represented the view that deeds can be made definite, that they can be part of a predetermined pattern. If the law is seen in any other terms it ceases to have religious validity.

At this point Rosenzweig's analogy of the law to teachings becomes crucial. Buber would have responded to Rosenzweig that seen from his perspective the details of the law, its particular content, may well represent an immediate and spontaneous response to God. Still, the perspective which produces that impression of the law's content is identical with one that finds in the law *only teachings*. The law is in fact reduced from legislation to a cultural manifestation of God's communication with man. Buber would agree with this but he would hesitate to call such a view legalistic.

Is the problem involved anything more than a linguistic one? While Buber might argue that Rosenzweig overlooks the fact that the content of the law understood as teachings can and certainly does lead to a spontaneous response to God, is he merely quibbling? Buber's positive approach to ritual and rules might be seen as a tacit agreement with Rosenzweig. His objections may be entirely verbal and thereby theoretically indefensible. Buber's view can be defended as an attempt to preserve the integrity of three different strands within Judaism. Only when those three strands are kept apart as independent forces does the dynamics of Jewish life become comprehensible. Such a defense would require a full-scale investigation of Jewish history. Given the intellectual background of Buber's exchange with Rosenzweig we can ask a more limited question: Does Buber's analysis refute the Spinozan-Mendelssohnian reduction of Judaism to legalism more effectively than the alternative systems of his own era? Does his rejection of Rosenzweig's proposals reflect a superior theological option rather than merely a subjective response? After examining what Buber means when he divides Judaism into three component parts—deed, teachings, and the law—we will be better able to answer this question.

Judaism's "Deed-Tendency"

Buber finds one of Judaism's most characteristic features to be a concern for the concrete, bodily expression of religion. The meaning of faith is communicated by deeds rather than by dogmas. This orientation to action is not exclusively Jewish. Buber finds it a peculiarity of Oriental religion in general. Whereas the Occidental will abstract general principles as the basis of religion, the Eastern personality, he suggests, prefers to define faith by the way in which life is shaped:

> the Jew is endowed with greater motor than sensory faculties . . . he considers doing more essential than experiencing . . . not faith but deed was central to Jewish religiosity. This conception may in fact be viewed as the fundamental difference between Orient and Occident: for the Oriental the decisive bond between man and God is the deed, for the Occidental, faith.[23]

At first glance Buber's remarks seem addressed to the question of religion: What is the primary mode of religious life? Yet note that Buber has an alternate definition of deed. Whereas deed in ordinary thought refers to any action, any physical motion of the individual, Buber claims that a deed is a *religiously relevant act*. The very requirements for deed performance change when seen in this way. If a deed is the bond between man and God, then any act which fails to live up to this expectation is unworthy of being accepted as a deed. Action which does not take God seriously as part of the context of doing fails to become a deed. How does the individual take God seriously as part of the context of action? What concrete difference is entailed between performing an act and engaging in a religious deed? The religious dimension of a deed stems from its subjective meaning. It is performed from a total and genuine response to the situation as a whole, to the historical demands of the moment. The religious nature of this response arises from the subject's recognition that God makes infinite demands on every individual in accordance with the historical context in which the individual exists. Since God is both infinite and concerned with history, every historical moment contains infinite commands specific to itself. The religious individual performs all his deeds out of an awareness that each moment is a moment of revelation. Each deed is also an existential risk—the risk of misunderstanding God's commands issuing from the situation. The consequences of a deed point beyond themselves to God's infinite and eternal plan. Man's act affects not only its immediate context but also the totality of the divine scheme of history. The subjective willingness of the individual or group engaging in an act to stake its life and meaning on the authenticity of its response to God, on the accuracy of its deed as a fulfillment of the commands of the hour, can determine the religious quality of a deed.

Nations as well as individuals can perform deeds. A nation can accept a collective task, a national and cultural mission, which is appropriate to and called forth by the divine command in history. As with the individual, so too this communal deed performance must be performed with the totality of life. For a nation that means with all the economic, political, and cultural aspects of its civilization. There are, thus, two aspects of the religious deed:

> It must in the first place, comprise the whole life, the whole civilization of a people, economy, society, and state; and secondly, it must incorporate the whole of the individual, his emotions and his will, his actions and abstentions, his life at home and in the market place, in the temple and in the popular assembly.[24]

Because the individual and the community invest the deed with the totality of their being and risk their meaning when they perform it, a deed signifies more than its immediate effects. It represents the tradition and pattern of life from which it came. It is the culmination of motivations, of preparation, of the history that preceded it. A deed always points beyond itself to the future. A deed suggests the direction of future deeds, the future meaning of the individual and the nation, the future possibilities for decision-making. "Something infinite," Buber comments, "flows into a deed of a man; something infinite flows from it." A religious deed is characterized by an awareness of this infinite significance of action. Those religions which cultivate the "deed-tendency" do so not because they value this or that act, not because they consecrate this or that isolated activity, but because they are aware of the infinite meaning of all actions. The deed-conscious individual is one who humbly asserts his ignorance of the total meaning of his actions, who cannot fathom the full significance of his deeds, but who "must nevertheless be aware that the fullness of the world's destiny, namelessly interwoven, passes through his hands."[25]

Just because a person never knows the infinite causes and consequences interwoven in his deed, religious action always entails a risk. Together with the demand that he stake his whole being on his act an individual needs to have a basic religious trust. The prophets are the best representatives of such trust. They recognize the total risk they run, the infinite task that confronts them, but because of their rootedness in a divine trust they persevere. The fruit of their struggles and the basic element in any deed is the messianic hope.[26] A religious deed always indicates a decision made out of the messianic vision, out of a trust in the divine and his hopes for man's future. The messianic vision always stands as a corrective to those among mankind who assume that all tasks have been accomplished, all aims achieved. These men think that their own actions are self-sufficient; they know what is required and feel they can fulfill every need. In contrast to such omnipotence the messianic vision constantly criticizes the status quo. It prevents the elevation of this or that act to the status of an eternal truth. All efforts to substitute one or another human action as an unchanging religious deed are challenged by the messianic vision. No action is complete until the final fulfillment. All actions are merely passing, momentary stages linking the past and future.

Both the messianic consciousness and the subjective risking of one's total being refer to the person performing the deed rather than to the deed itself. Attitude rather than content determines the religious value of the deed. Two people can perform the same action, make identical physical gestures, but one can do so as the means to a purely human goal and without a wider awareness of the infinitude present in his act, while the second can be making the motions of religious trust, risking his total being. Thus Buber claims that "Not the matter of a deed determines its truth but the manner in which it is carried out: in human conditionality, or in divine unconditionality."[27]

How does Buber justify his claim that Jewish religiosity is characterized by the deed tendency? The Bible, he suggests, demonstrates this view. If this is the case, how are the various legal passages to be explained? Apparently the biblical authors felt that the content of the law as well as its attitude was essential. The law seems to point to specific tasks, demanding particular obligations. These can be explained as vehicles for deed performance. Their specific content derives from man's need to concretize the deed tendency. Their religious value transcends their content and resides in the opportunities they present for meeting the unconditioned demand of the situation. "Dogmas and rules," for Buber, "are merely the result subject to change, of the human mind's endeavor to make comprehensible, by a symbolic order of the knowable and doable, the working of the unconditional it experiences within itself." Biblical legislation is a reflection on the unconditioned meeting between man and God's command in the situation. Its laws and statutes do not imply a legalism but rather a responsive ritualism. They are specific guideposts to an encounter with the divine command in the present. Certain biblical critics confused the deed-tendency evidenced in these laws with a sterile legalism. They "assumed that this means a soulless glorification of works or rituals devoid of inner significance; on the contrary every deed, even the smallest and seemingly most negligible, is in some way oriented toward the divine."[28]

Such an interpretation of the legal traditions imbedded in the Bible can be found in prophetic and Hasidic Judaism. These movements were expressive protests against an excessive legalism—a fact that Buber never forgets. The deed-tendency is characteristically in tension with legalism. As true religiosity expressing Judaism's spontaneous response to the divine, it often contradicts the formalized "religion" of the Jewish leadership. The prophetic denunciation of priestly religion is a case in point. The prophet calls Israel to decision-making. He opposes the cult, not as ritual, but in its pretended self-sufficiency. God, the prophet announces, does not desire the specific content of religious ritualism. The social and personal consequences of taking a risk in the realm of history are for him the primary religious move. The prophet castigates "religion" because "God does not attach decisive importance to 'religion.' . . . He desires no religion, He desires a human people, men living together, the makers of decisions vindicating their right to those thirsting for justice."[29] The prophet does not reject ritual as such. His quarrel is not with the content of "religion" but with its tendency to divert attention from the primary issues: the consequences of deed performance. From Moses onward, Buber argues, prophets recognized the need for religious forms. A structure of religious rituals helps educate a people in God's desires; it provides occasions on which an individual can feel the address of God in history more directly and explicitly than ordinarily. Moses as lawmaker is no way contradictory to Moses as prophet if law is not taken as an end in itself but as a means of pointing the way toward deed performance. God's command to man is communicated

> not merely by means of instantaneous decisions but also through lasting justice and law. . . . for without law, that is without any clear-cut and transmissible line of demarcation between that which is pleasing to God and that which is displeasing to Him, there can be no historical continuity of divine rule on earth.[30]

Law here does not imply an unchanging legislation but rather an institutionalized way of communicating God's demand for deeds. Scholars misunderstand Joshua's "covenant ceremony" when they see it as establishing a constitution, or new legal system in Israel. Joshua's covenant is different in quality from that given at Sinai. It reaffirms the need for deed even in the midst of obedience to the law. Israel had followed God's law but had not done so exclusively. The influence of the Canaanites had stimulated additions to the Israelite cult. Joshua demands a present decision for God as well as the continuation of past legal precepts. Joshua's response to Israel represented "his experience as leader of the people and their commander," and his call was not to legal observance but to historical responsiveness.[31]

Hasidism as well as prophecy provides Buber with an example of the deed-tendency in tension with other elements in Jewish life. The prophet spoke against cult as an artificial act, a deed without historical validity. Hasidism addressed a sacramental legalism that had been divorced from the historical demands that had called it forth. Both prophets and Hasidic leaders addressed "the man in a situation of this man's present power of decision."[32] Hasidism called for the active deed, the decision in life, of which the prophets had spoken. The process by which cult had dissociated itself from deed and set itself up as an independent religious truth was repeated in the late medieval legalistic tradition. There this process was recognizable in the growing estrangement between the dynamics of individual life and the communal structure of Jewish authority. Obedience to rabbinical leaders replaced daily decision-making. The legal codes were set apart as the only true religious guide, the only valid religious act. Buber's interpretation of medieval history is without doubt highly subjective. Many scholars would oppose his view of the development of Jewish religion. Nevertheless this schema is the indispensable background for Buber's interpretation of Hasidism. Hasidism reacted to legalism just as prophecy responded to the priestly cult. The prophets, it will be recalled, did not oppose the cult as such but rather its claim to represent the totality of religious truth. The Hasidim did not oppose Jewish law but its self-identification with the whole of Judaism. As a continuation of the deed-tendency in Judaism Hasidism represents the true meaning of "sacramental existence":

> To the man of sacramental existence no kind of acquired rules and rhythms, no inherited method of working avail, nothing "known," nothing "learned"; he has to withstand ever again the unforeseen, unforeseeable moment, ever again to extend liberation, fulfillment to a thing or being that he meets in the moment flowing toward him.[33]

In Hasidism ritualism returns to the originally fluid form of sacramentalism which characterized prophetic religion but was later transformed into legalism. Religious observance became for the Hasid a vehicle by which the deed could be performed. Since in its essential nature Jewish practice is merely a collection of opportunities for decision, Hasidism had no need to reject the law. Buber, however, is restless with Hasidism's compromise with the legal tradition. Hasidism's critique of legalism is less impetuous than that of prophecy. Although Hasidism demanded that all sacramental actions enjoined by the law become alive as present moments of decision, it was less creative than prophecy. While creative within the law, Hasidism did not create beyond the law. By rejuvenating the law, Hasidism also justified its reluctance to change and augment the legal tradition. Buber finds the identification of deed with the authentic performance of the law a fatal error. While the law can become a source for deeds, deeds naturally expand beyond the province of the law. If such expansion is not allowed, if the intrinsic difference between law and deed is overlooked, the way is open for stagnation. Legalism has an easy time establishing control over the deed-tendency and reducing a spontaneous response to God to a superficial and I-It type of manipulative action. Thus Buber explains:

> it is understandable why Hasidism had no incentive to break loose any stick from the structure of the traditional Law, for according to

the Hasidic teaching there could not exist anything that was not to be fulfilled with intention or whose intention could not be discovered. But it is also understandable how just thereby the conserving force secretly remained superior to the moving and renewing one and finally conquered it within Hasidism itself.[34]

Judaism is a religion in tension, and unless this tension is acknowledged even the most deed-oriented impulses can be overpowered.

The same tension exists in modern Jewish life. The Zionist movement seeks to demonstrate its connection with the Jewish past. Buber notes that a return to older patterns can be either a false reverence or a false façade hiding radical discontinuity. Tradition can, it is true, be an essential ingredient in a modern movement of renewal. As the basis for a sensitivity to God's demands in the present, the Jewish past can be the foundation for a rebirth of Judaism. Buber rejected Ahad HaAm's vision of cultural renewal. A spiritual center based upon past ethics can be a scholarly or propagandistic influence. It cannot cultivate a living confrontation with the present hour in all its immediacy. Decision-making and deed performance are possible only when man meets his historical situation with an honest openness. A study of tradition can awaken this type of honesty and thereby "beget the only things from which I expect the absolute to emerge—return and transformation, and a change in all elements in life."[35]

The Jewish tradition, in all its complexity and diversity, despite its tendency toward legalism, is an appropriate means of stimulating spiritual renewal. In conveying the deed-tendency Buber looks to the tradition as an illustration of ways in which Jews have responded religiously to the historical expression of God's commands. Jewish history is exemplary, not because it represents the perfection of the deed-tendency, but because the history of the struggles undergone by movements such as prophecy and Hasidism can stimulate similar struggles in the present. Buber educates his generation by appealing to the Jewish past. Education demands neither an imitation of that past nor any single ideological point of view. Buber advocates a type of education that is a preparation for spontaneous response. He seeks: "The education that leads man to a lived connection with his world and enables him to ascend from there to faithfulness, to standing the test, to authenticating, to responsibility, to decision, to realization." Such an education demands openness. The individual cannot prejudge the tradition. All of its elements—the prophetic and the priestly, the Hasidic and the legalistic—must be confronted honestly. The educational process is stifled if *a priori* decisions control the flexibility of the learning situation. Both teacher and student need to explore the entire range of Jewish living if their study is to awaken an authentic response. The law viewed as a detailed list of prohibitions and prescriptions precludes Jewish learning. The law as a datum of Jewish experience is indispensable for it. In the process of education Buber holds freedom and openness to be the most basic prerequisites. The student seeks to perceive that within the tradition which stimulates present response. One, however, "who does not allow the inner selection and formation to prevail, but instead inserts an aim from the beginning, has forfeited the meaning of this perception."[36]

The Teachings of Judaism

Buber's view of Jewish education brings us back to *I and Thou*. Education for responsive living preserves that vital religiosity which animates true religion. Teaching, as we have seen before, is the true aim of religious art, literature, and ritual. Teaching as the realization of spirit in human life necessarily demands dynamic change and growth. No person is so rigid that he does not develop; a personal religiosity, then, must be a developing one. Ritual is teaching if it aims beyond itself into human lives. The purpose of ritual as teaching is to direct personal concerns and community awareness toward a fulfilled human life. Ritual recalls the basic task of self-fulfillment through self-risk, that is through entering an undetermined relationship. Ritual, as teaching, has a constructive purpose: it builds a human world in which living persons and relationships between them are the central values of both individual and communal concern. Such a view is already intimated in *I and Thou:*

> The anchoring of time in a relation-oriented life of salvation and the anchoring of space in a community unified by a common center: only when both of these come to be and only as long as both continue to be, a human cosmos comes to be and continues to be around the invisible altar, grasped in the spirit out of the world stuff of the eon.[37]

Religion establishes a world of relationship; its rituals enable meeting between men. These ends can be achieved only if rituals anchor both time and space to relationship and community. Such rituals arise from within history and must reflect that history. Buber rejects the view that rituals are unchanging. Yet he admits that behind ritual change—both the varying content and meaning ascribed to ritual performance and its method, utilizing ancient forms and symbols but transforming their import by creating many various styles—lies a common religious intuition. This intuition is neither identified with historical events nor separated from them; it is rather that "a relationship . . . embodies itself in a concrete event, which continues to operate concretely."[38] From *I and Thou* we learn that ritual must both incorporate history and transcend it, must be eternal in its impetus to change and representative of a particular moment in its form. In order to be true to this basic characteristic of living ritual a religious practice must be both dynamic and static at the same time. It must be dynamic insofar as it is part of a process; it must be static because it was called forth by man's need for a stoppage in time, for a resting place, a concrete embodiment of that changing process.

Rituals as creative teachings can now be evaluated. Such rituals are different from deeds: they convey the reality of deed symbolically but are the aftermath rather than the substance of deed. They are different from law: law claims to be eternal, unchanging, always valid; ritual claims only to be a historical manifestation of a changing process. Ritual as teaching communicates a continuity of purpose expressed through a variety of concrete expressions. Rituals such as these point beyond themselves to newly created ritualism. New and varied concrete responses are stimulated by the example of traditional ones. Creative ritual is evocative: it provokes continuing and innovative concretizations of men's on-going encounters. Each generation learns from ritual that lives are shaped by relationship, and each generation evolves new rituals to pass on the living inspiration for relationship. Buber finds in Judaism an example of this process. The tension between law and deed as revealed in ritual as teaching points, according to him, to the presence in Judaism of creative ritualism. Cult as teaching becomes cult as law and then demands revitalization. Buber finds in this cycle a confirmation of his analysis of religion in *I and Thou.*

One illustration of such creative teachings is found in the later chapters of the book of Isaiah. While these final chapters, so-called Second Isaiah, reveal a totally new historical setting, they also demonstrate a loving continuity of language, message, and concerns. As Buber envisions the situation, a disciple of the prophet Isaiah treasured his master's words in his heart. Learning them repeatedly he inevitably applied them to his new and unique historical situation. Spontaneously he discovers in these teachings a new message—one addressed to his time and place. The teachings become the occasion of a new spiritual event. Creative hearing of the documents of the past becomes a religious experience of the present.

The disciple hears faithfully; that is, he always hears without prejudgment: "every morning perceiving anew the message of his master in its true sense."[39] Not only Second Isaiah but the entire prophetic tradition evokes such a flexible creativity. The prophets emphasize the dynamic, spontaneous, and responsive nature of the tradition. They use traditional lore, myth, and legend to establish the context in which man can make decisions in the present. When rewriting primal history the prophets recast the original narratives. The origin of man as well as the origin of the Hebrew people becomes for them the basis of every man's power of decision. The past is used as a stimulus for decision-making in current times. The narratives of Genesis, for example, seem to Buber examples of an attempt at

> anchoring in the origin mystery the unalienable right of revelation and its irreducible sense against the claims of a myth and ritual that had become independent, that is to say to prove that every creation, foundation, blessing, commandment, judgment, punishment, election, assistance, and covenant-making in early history is a kind of revelation. According to the intention this cannot be done by laying down certain theological propositions . . . the teaching must be nothing other than narrative history.[40]

Teachings by their nature cannot be reduced to dogmas or theology. They offer no final conclusions, no ultimate answers. They point to a way, illustrate possible alternatives, and refuse any effort to construe them as final, decisive, or all-inclusive.

Just as the prophetic word points beyond any concrete narrative, so the prophetic act conceives of religious gesture as a changing, on-going process. The cultic rite becomes teaching insofar as it remains a flexible instrument reflecting and responding to the historical situation. Cult as prophetic act is as much teaching as the prophetic word. In prophecy every deed takes on a symbolic meaning: "Not only his organs of speech but the whole man is taken up into the service of the spirit. The body and life of the man become a part of this service, and by this a symbol of the message."[41] Living ritual born out of historical reality is part of teaching because it represents one possible concretization of man's response to the demands of God articulated in history.

This responsive ritualism must be distinguished from priestly cult. Priestly cult aims at timelessness and eternity. Prophetic ritual always stands ready for the intrusion of the new word of God which "comes again and again from heaven as something new . . . [and] suddenly descends into the human situation, unexpected and unwilled by man."[42] As with the word, so ritual has two aspects. As a record of spontaneous gesture it inspires dynamic religiousness. But if its content is elevated to an absolute status it obstructs the religious intuition. Any attempt at imitation of ritual undermines its creative power. Man can emulate the ritual response of the past, but if he seeks to duplicate this or that ritual action he necessarily fails to cultivate true religiosity. Prophetic gestures were unique to their historical setting. Viewed dynamically these gestures can evoke new rituals. Viewed statically prophetic example declines into priestly, imitative cultic performance.

Cult, when used in this connection, refers to an organized, routine, and established ritual system. It includes making sacrifices, chanting hymns, reciting prayers, and following detailed procedures for personal behavior. Cult refers to the established way to behaving toward the divine. Cult is not necessarily an evil phenomenon. Buber constantly reminds his readers that the I-Thou encounter is transient. Since the encounter cannot last, cult is created as a vehicle for its return. The priestly leadership acts as guide and partner helping individuals step into relationship with nature, other people, and spiritual creations. The festival calendar, the ritual require- ments, the sacrificial offerings of a religious tradition serve as the framework within which encounter can take place. Only when a cult loses sight of its true purpose—which is to serve encounter and not to replace it—does it become a force of decay and stagnation in a culture.

Israel's festal calendar, its original cult, was prophetic in essence. Moses enjoins ritual performance as a means of demonstrating God's concern for every aspect of life. A comprehensive ritualism communicates the divine interest in the totality of human existence. Such a cult ensures that Israel's God "does not become the lord of a cultic order of faith, shut up within itself, but the lord of an order of people including all spheres of life."[43] Mosaic ritual is indicative rather than exhaustive. The Decalogue, for example, speaks only of the Sabbath; it does not give a detailed description of the major festivals, and even Sabbath observance is merely suggested and not legislated in minute details. God's concern with time and space is the primary lesson taught, not a specific code of law. Religious principles rather than cultic particularity are emphasized: "The cult is not in any way excluded, but only its general prerequisite postulates, as they are expressed in the first part of the Decalogue, and not its details, have found acceptance here, in accordance with the main purpose."[44]

Because the teachings abstract general ideals from historical examples, they point to an endless series of concrete realizations. They provide the ground for further deed performance. Yet deed and teaching must be separated as two different phenomena. Deed can be performed without recourse to the teachings. Buber fears such an approach: false deeds are too easily allowed to penetrate the realm of religion. The man of today, he suggests, is often so eager to take an existential risk, to experience the religious depth of deed performance, that his religious spirit falls into sentiment and false religiosity. In his eagerness for experience the modern man fails to be sensitive to the historical situation and God's commands found within it. Deed performance is composed of both decision itself and deciding based upon an acknowledgment of God's unconditioned address. The ear of man, however, needs to be sensitized to that divine voice. In the midst of history's confused cacophony of sounds, only the trained ear can discern the divine command. Orientation to deed without the training of the teachings can produce demonic as well as godly actions. "We live in an age," Buber declares, "when deeds tend to assert their superiority over the teachings." He insists on both the independence and the necessity of both elements. Deeds are never substitutes for the teachings. Entering into deed performance does not excuse the individual from the obligation of turning to the teachings. Jews, Buber admits, are restless with the restrictions placed upon them by tradition. They seek a new religious vitality. Buber sympathizes with this aim, but denies that it entails a rejection of the teachings. Despite their association with Jewish legalism, the teachings are not the law. They do not usurp the deed-tendency of its centrality. There is no need to negate the teachings in order to insure the primacy of deed. "The teachings," Buber told his auditors at the Frankfurt Lehrhaus in 1934, "do not center in themselves; they do not exist for their own sake. They refer to, they are directed toward the deed."[45] While separate, then, deed and teachings are intrinsically related to each other. Both stand in contrast to a crystallization of the past as an object of imitation; both oppose and are opposed by the legalist tradition in Judaism.

The Crystallization of Judaism in Law

Deed and teachings point beyond themselves; they demand continually new concretizations of religiosity. Law, by contrast, exalts the past. It presents religion with a crystallization of history in specific forms which are meant to be imitated throughout eternity without regard to history. Unlike the deed, law requires no risk. The meaning of each legislated act is fully determined. Because its content never changes its consequences are likewise held constant. A deed is at the mercy of its results and implications; a legal action has no historical consequences, only eternal implications. The teachings remain open to changes and stimulate development. Law, however, depends upon faithful imitation of an original deed. Law proposes an eternal pattern, revealed once in history and repeated thereafter as an unchanging supra-historical duty. The content of ritual rather than its intention is the paradigm for legalism. Even in its most exalted form legalism finds internal motivation to be associated with, if not identical to, external performance. The same motivation that stimulated the original deed is supposedly repeated whenever the deed is reconstructed through ritual action.

The law is thus a content, set for all time and established as an unchanging response to the divine. Legalism in itself, however, is an attitude. The very same acts and precepts that evoke responsive deeds when interpreted as teachings prevent religiosity when understood as law. The content which legalism elevates to the status of eternal truth is the same content by which the teachings stimulate new religious forms. Legalism is an approach to the Jewish past, an approach which sees that past as "something finished and univocal." That unchangeable pattern exalted by the law, however, can just as easily be interpreted as passing manifestations of the human ability to answer God's historical challenges. While legalism opposes the teachings, the content of the law can be viewed positively. An unfinished tale can be derived from the examples of legalism: "the living religious forces which, though active and manifest in all of Jewish religion, in its teaching and its law, have not been fully expressed by either."[46] The precepts and statutes of the law can provide a vehicle for religious forces. Legalism as such can only block the religious process since its identification of past manifestations of religiosity as immutable, eternal truths prevent further development of the religious spirit.

The legalist interpretation of Judaism found an articulate spokesman in Samson Raphael Hirsch. Even Buber conceded the authenticity of Hirsch's approach to the content of Judaism. Such a concession may be rooted in Hirsch's opposition to external "ceremony"—an antipathy shared by Buber. Hirsch condemns behavioralism, an attitude that finds in Jewish observances merely a pattern of action sanctioned by the past, ceremonially impressive, but spiritually sterile. He claims that the only valid rationale for Jewish observance is the conviction that these actions set down in the past are eternal demands by the divine. Only the recognition that the law is an accurate transcription of the desires of God provides a truly religious motivation for Jewish religious living. Hirsch bases his call to traditional Jewish action on the assumption that the tradition in all its details can be identified with God's "sacred, eternal, and solemn will."[47] Buber can understand and even appreciate the religious honesty represented by this view. However, he also notes that this idea leads inevitably to a loss of spontaneity. For example, Hirsch divides reality into two spheres: that of social life—*derech eretz*—where demands are always changing and that of *Torah,* unchanging religious demands. While Hirsch does argue that the two are interrelated, Torah always has the task of molding *derech eretz*. God's demands do not change in response to history; the means for implementing Torah merely undergoes revision. The basic religious intuition that action must be based on confidence in God's revelation and not in any extrinsic motivation is shared by both the teachings and the law. The law, however, implies a continuity of aims as well as a continuity of religious insight. The teachings inspire new modes of behavior; the law discourages any change from the past.

The teachings, as Buber sees them, emphasize that man can never know God's nature, that his recognition of the divine command is always limited. Man cannot, "therefore, understand what directly or indirectly (be it through written or oral tradition) proceeds from the factual revelation."[48] Hirsch counters this claim by stating that the only knowledge necessary is that God has revealed his will in this law. While Buber uses the teachings to show men grappling with the divine, Hirsch sees in that same content an exhaustive list of God's commands. All man needs to know is that God has provided him with a blueprint for action and that by following that blueprint he "is thereby performing God's will and so fulfilling his vocation as a man and an Israelite."[49] From the standpoint of the teachings the equation of the knowable with past knowledge is stifling. In a phrase that seems to echo Hirsch's view of Torah and *derech eretz,* Buber finds the glorification of the past as an unchanging and independent reality to be an "amputation" of "lived everyday" life such that "life in the world and the service of God run side by side without connection."[50] The difference between deed and law is that deed maintains the importance of this moment, the spontaneous response called forth by history, while law enshrines past behavior as ultimate; it is the only authentic form of action. The difference between the teachings and law is similar. The teachings see the past as an example for the future, as motivation for innovation in the present. The law sets up the past as a paradigm for all activity, as the only religious alternative for present individuals. For the teachings the Jewish past illustrates the creative union of history and command; for the law that past represents an intrusion of the divine into the dynamic and changing stage of human history.

Buber found the contrast and conflict between these two approaches to a religious past deeply rooted in Jewish history. The cultic calendar and its development demonstrate this deep-seated tension. Originally the holidays recalled holy moments of the past and inspired moments akin to them in the present. The festivals were frameworks within which spiritual renewal occurred: "Something had happened to Israel which in the cycle of the seasons became the core of its life of faith to think of again and again."[51] Festivals were opportunities for a renewal through standing in direct relationship and responsiveness with God. Memory served to stimulate present deed performance. Buber sees Solomon as a crucial transition figure. By associating the cult with kingship, he reduced its power and scope. The royal celebrations become the means of fulfilling all of Israel's religious obligations. The king represents religion through his role in the cult; he stands for expediency in his political program. The festivals become nationalistic expressions of a self-satisfied religious arrogance. In Solomon, Buber explains, "we meet the unreserved expression of the aim of the early Kingdom to confine YHVH's sovereignty within the cultic sphere alone."[52]

Law is no less antithetical to the teachings than it is to the deed. This opposition springs from the competition between law and teachings for the same content: statutes, wisdom, narrative, and poetry. The teachings demand that the content be viewed as a vehicle stimulating change. The law inevitably confronts this claim with its affirmation of the sanctity and unchanging nature of the content itself. The law finds its authority undermined by the teachings; the teachings find their purpose thwarted by the law. How is it that the two can tolerate one another so that there is an uneasy coexistence? The teachings can recognize in the law an institution for preserving the memory of past deeds; while the law must be transcended, its practical function can be tolerated. The law, on the other hand, can reinterpret the teaching, can bend it to its own purpose. Buber remarks that much that we now find within Scriptures came there through misinterpretation, "probably not unintentionally, by the law-observing redactors of the canon."[53] Such compromises did not lead to a symbiosis such as that between deed and teaching, but did insure a continuous tension between the two elements. Jewish history is complex just because these elements did not defeat each other. Both have a characteristic place within Judaism.

Law, Ritual, and I and Thou

The clue to Buber's stance against both Hirsch and Rosenzweig lies in his attitude toward religious evolution. *I and Thou* establishes the pattern: response followed by crystallization leading to renewal. Unlike Hirsch, then, Buber cannot accept the law as a final and eternal truth. Yet unlike Rosenzweig he cannot acknowledge the "command" as the basic category. *I and Thou* sets the stage for a mediating view: Judaism is inevitably a religion of tension. The core of any religiosity is always an immediate relationship with the divine. All ritual, however, can only be a human reflection of that relationship. Such ritual inevitably becomes frozen as law and this very development is an impetus to developing new forms! Buber's response to Rosenzweig is part of his total understanding of Jewish ritual and reflects his belief in the cyclical pattern of religious practices. While Hirsch represents one pole of Judaism, Rosenzweig represents its opposite. Neither are true to the religious dynamics which Buber discovered in *I and Thou*. Buber emphasizes the independence of Judaism's three components—teachings, law, and deed. A Judaism based only on law subjects all ritualism to the authority of the past. A Judaism based on responsiveness alone stimulates new ritualism, but ignores the tension basic to religious life. It fatally disregards the dynamics which will change even its responsive living into frozen law. By refusing to equate deed-consciousness and teachings Buber was forced to reject Rosenzweig's proposal to call the law "commandment." This rejection reflects and expands the insight into religious development first outlined in *I and Thou*.

Chapter III
Buber's Zionism

Zionism and Jewish Religion

Buber and Rosenzweig seem to reverse positions when we turn from the issue of ritual to that of Zionism. It is now Buber's turn to pose the question. Why should Rosenzweig have remained so passive a Zionist? Although our study is focused on Buber, a comparison between Buber and Rosenzweig is useful nonetheless since Rosenzweig represents a religiously based ambivalence to Zionism, an ambivalence Buber, as we shall see, shares. Rosenzweig did not take the step of active commitment to Zionism yet Buber did, and we must ask why. Buber certainly agreed with Rosenzweig that Zionism could become idolatrous and lead away from vital Jewish religiosity. Rosenzweig did not reject Buber's sense of Zion's centrality in Judaism. Rosenzweig, like Buber, recognized the danger of Zionism's becoming a substitute for living religious response: "All recipes, whether Zionist, orthodox, or liberal, produce caricatures of men, that become more ridiculous the more closely the recipes are followed." If Zionism is a recipe, then what is its caricature? Rosenzweig sees Zionism losing its spiritual and religious power by descending into crass materialism. As a political opportunism Zionism is a caricature, a recipe that has grown stale. How can Zionism retain its spontaneity, escape the danger of caricature? Rosenzweig replies that only by adhering to spiritual homelessness even if they are seeking a physical home can they remain true to Jewish religion. In order to "hold fast to their *goal* . . .

they must be homeless in time and remain wanderers, even there." Here is Buber's demand for creative response given a different form. That Rosenzweig shares Buber's view of process becomes clear in his admission of the merits of Zionism. "What religion needs," Rosenzweig comments, "is spontaneity! And when I consider what has spontaneously arisen in Palestine, I must admit that nowhere in the world have the demands of Jewish religious liberalism been met, even today, as fully as there." It is not surprising that Rosenzweig demanded the right of the Jews to have a land of their own. He vigorously defended this right against that view which completely spiritualized the concepts of Israel and Zion: "If a symbol is to be more than an arbitrary appendage, then it must somewhere and somehow exist as an entirely asymbolic reality."[1]

Rosenzweig's religiousness was close to Buber's yet it did not lead him to an active Zionism. This should warn us against making hasty judgments about Buber's Zionism. His religious restlessness with recipes, with unchallenged visions, with easy solutions was no less than Rosenzweig's. Merely because he was a religious radical, however, does not imply an active Zionism—Rosenzweig makes that clear. Buber differs from Rosenzweig by finding in it not a political program but a framework for social and political transformation. Why could Buber view it that way but not Rosenzweig? Perhaps the answer lies in Buber's emphasis on the concrete symbol. To have reality a symbol must be present bodily as well as spiritually; it must be realized as physical reality as well as intellectual truth. This theology of symbolism certainly informed Buber's political action. Although theologically Rosenzweig's views were very similar to Buber's, Rosenzweig was never moved to political activism in defense of Zionism.

To discover the roots of Buber's Zionism we must look beyond his demand for spontaneity and his rejection of recipes, beyond his view of Jewish religiosity as process, beyond his symbolic realism.

S. H. Bergman is correct when he implies a direct relationship between Buber's political thinking and his I-Thou philosophy. Bergman describes his own experience when confronted by Buber's early addresses on Judaism. Not only did the message of those words—the Jewish concern with unity and the universal implication of that concern—strike him; the method and presence of the speaker addressed him directly. The addresses were an example of dialogic living put into practice.[2] Buber's concern with social organization in general and with Zionism in particular is rooted in dialogic philosophy.

Having noticed this religious orientation in Buber's Zionism, we must acknowledge that Buber himself and most of his critics and expositors notice it as well. The discussion that follows proceeds in well-established paths. What is important to remember, however, is that Buber's Zionism, while predating *I and Thou,* was also shaped by it. This chapter does not offer new insights into Buber's Zionism; well-trodden paths have already marked out the way to discover the religious element in it. By introducing this restatement of Buber's Zionism with the relevant chapters in *I and Thou,* however, that work may gain in meaning. Buber's musing on man's twofold construction of reality is not merely philosophy or anthropology. The reader has missed an important dimension in the work if he overlooks its sociological thrust. The real advantage of following our exposition of *I and Thou* with a recapitulation of Buber's thinking on social issues and Zionism is to demonstrate that these latter are commentaries on the former. *I and Thou* is a document of Jewish faith precisely because Buber saw that faith as inevitably social.

It is easy to underestimate the social significance of *I and Thou.* Buber dwells on institutions and community as illustrations of the basic dichotomy of human life. His emphasis on a divine center for communal living almost escapes notice. The general theme of man's existence, the specific concerns with freedom and fate, with the gates of relationship, and with the "melancholy of our fate" obscure the social importance of Buber's paragraphs on social structures. If we isolate these paragraphs and bring them together, we will note a developing concern: from institutional life as an illustration of the human dilemma Buber moves to a consideration of authentic communal life. The major principles of Buber's social thinking need to be established. Three stand out as central themes in *I and Thou:* first the limitations together with the challenge of institutions, second the meaning of community, and finally the religious necessity for community. After we collate these passages in *I and Thou,* their meaning can be deepened by reference to Buber's Zionist writing.

The Meaning of Religious Community

Despite the decided influence of Kierkegaard on his thought, Buber returns again and again to his restlessness with the Dane's "Solitary One."[3] His disquiet is evident in *I and Thou.* The view of religious man as a solitary being who can dispense with relationships to the world is rejected as untenable. Buber recognizes the root of such a view. Individuals are uneasy with institutions. Communal life seems to engulf them. He has his "Speaker" ask, "But isn't the communal life of modern man bound to be submerged in the It-world?" The question is a genuine one. Modern men find their spiritual identity in conflict with an institutionalized world that levels all identities. Buber's first task is to reinstate communal life as a truly religious phenomenon. He opposes the separation of "feelings" and "institutions" as if "private" and "public" life could be split between them. Of course institutions do not create "public life." Just as clearly "feelings" do not create "private life." Both feelings and institutions are unreal and false because they are separated: "The severed It of institutions is a golem and the severed I of feelings is a fluttering soul-bird. Neither knows the human being. . . . Neither knows person or community." Persons and community are dependent upon neither feelings nor institutions but upon the right relationship of men to each other and the world. The dichotomy between institutions and feelings, between public and private life, is misleading. What is needed is not a rejection of public life, not a cultivation of inwardness, but responsive living in which inner and outer are equally valid components in a full life. "True public and true personal life," he explains, "are two forms of association."[4] Buber is facing a basic problem in modern Jewish existence: how to recapture religious authenticity. Buber opposes those who advocate a withdrawal to personal introspection. Vital Jewish religiosity—both in the personal and public domains—is born of association, not of isolation. Those who look to feelings to produce the "loving community" are misled. And not institutions but persons are central. What must be changed is how men are, not how they fashion this or that social structure. The concern for solitary religiosity is, Buber contends, a problem in itself; it deflects from the real object of living—relationship.

Buber presents his view of religious community in direct contradiction to the "romantic" reliance on feelings. Not feelings but a common relationship creates community:

> True community does not come into being because people have feelings for each other (though that is required, too), but rather on two accounts: all of them have to stand in a living, reciprocal relationship to a single living center, and they have to stand in a living, reciprocal relationship to one another.[5]

The essential fact about community is that it grows organically around a common center. Individuals grow out of this common center and from it develop genuine and unique meetings with each other. What must be emphasized is that community is secondary. The stretching out to each other is a consequence of the original relationship with the center. "Not the periphery, not the community comes first, but the radii, the common relation to the center. That alone assures the genuine existence of a community."[6] Community is more than social structures; it represents a joining of persons rather than a created political body. While institutions and political programs are not unimportant—they can obstruct Thou-saying or lay the foundations for it—the central reality of community is independent of them.

Community grows out of You-saying. What then of its

structures? Buber certainly allows for the importance of institutions, but in a secondary role. He admits the necessity of communal forms, their indispensability. Because these forms provide the backdrop for all relationship they must be taken with utter seriousness. Institutions are the mundane tools of the Thou-world:

> Man's communal life cannot dispense any more than he himself with the It-world—over which the presence of the You floats like the spirit over the face of the waters. Man's will to profit and will to power are natural and legitimate as long as they are tied to the will to human relations and carried by it.[7]

Community, no less than personhood, is composite: originating in relationship it continues in existence because of forms and structures. The basic task is to preserve the originating impulse, the freedom and flexibility demanded if institutional forms are to be transformed back into living relationships. Such flexibility is not, according to Buber, unusual or esoteric. The ordinary conditions of modern business life provide opportunities for relationship.

What is required is that the concern for relationship be preserved. The statesman and the social leader have that very task. They are to organize society for the sake of encounter, to provide the framework in which meeting is made possible. Buber denies that service to this task makes one a "dilettante." A statesman or business leader engaged in this service "knows well that he cannot simply confront the people with whom he has to deal as so many carriers of the You, without undoing his own work." His role is not to exemplify You-saying every minute; Buber acknowledges that that is impossible. Instead such a social leader bears witness to the primacy of You-saying as the basis of social life. He maintains that "what is decisive is whether the spirit—the You-saying, responding spirit—remains alive and actual."[8] Preservation of this actuality is the basic concern of such a businessman who while involved necessarily in the I-It world must always look beyond it as well. Communal life is served best by those who are aware of their indispensable need for institutions, feelings, and the It-world, but who also keep alive that You-saying spirit which justifies I-It life as an opportunity for transformation into I-You being.

Community depends upon the possibility of You-sayings being exchanged between individuals who create and sustain group living. Because true community depends first on true personhood, which in turn depends upon the possibility of relationship, it implies a religious task. You-saying is made possible by the existence of an Eternal You whose very being cannot be transformed into an It. True community takes as its center nothing less than the Eternal You; the possibility of relationship is thereby established as the basis of communal life. That the Eternal You is the center of true community is implied but not stated in *I and Thou*. The Eternal You itself is the subject and concern of the third part of that work. We learn therein that "life with men" provides the language and speech which is the most developed form of relationship. It is in language that "what confronts us has developed the full actuality of the You."[9] Buber associates language with culture and society in other writings. In these works it becomes clear that human social life is essential for the development of an actualized You because such social life has God as its center.

Community, Buber writes elsewhere, "does not have its meaning in itself. It is the abode where the divine has not yet consumed itself, the abode of the coming theophany."[10] Community is an expectant arena waiting for divine revelation. Its meaning lies in its receptivity to the Eternal You. Man faces the challenge of recognizing the Eternal You; society and community are means by which he is strengthened to meet the challenge: "Even now a real decision is made in him, whether he faces the speech of God articulated to him in things and events—or escapes. And a creative glance towards his fellow-creature can at times suffice for response."[11] The significance of community is religious: it allows men to respond to the Eternal You. Community originates in a common relationship with the Eternal You and maintains itself by providing access to the

Eternal You. Both in beginning and in function, then, community is a religious phenomenon.

I and Thou *as Social Propaganda*

The discussion in *I and Thou* remains at an abstract level of philosophical theory. The reader would hardly guess that these issues of community and religious center motivated intense practical activity. Buber's involvement in both Socialism and Zionism prove the intensity of his practical concerns. However, Buber was skeptical of those who, like the political Zionists, hoped that the mighty world powers could through external and institutional means transform human communal life. He was skeptical of the Marxist claim that history itself would move relentlessly and impersonally to overcome man's inevitable alienation. Rather than rely on an invisible force which operates in I-It fashion, Buber trusted in I-Thou encounter as the basis of change. He was skeptical of "culture" and its institutions of education, folkways, and national customs which claimed to cultivate and stimulate communal identity. Only a lived relationship to a central Thou could create that vital identity which is born of I-Thou encounter. In the name of I-Thou existence Buber stood against the giants of Zionism, such as Theodor Herzl and David Ben-Gurion, advocating a Zionism of encounter rather than of politics.

The practical criticism that emerges from the principles touched on in *I and Thou* is, in its basic thrust, negative. Buber uses the positive vision of *I and Thou* as a means of rejecting social programs that fall short of his ideal. Both Socialists and Zionists placed their faith in transformed social institutions. New conditions of labor, new structures of social control and representation, new distributions of tasks and rewards formed the basis of their concerns. Buber took an adversary role against such proponents of this or that social change. Men, he contended, must be changed, not structures. Structures may facilitate human growth and spiritual rebirth; they cannot be a substitute for it. The glory of the fight for social improvement is not that the system has been changed, but that man's opportunities for true existence have been furthered. This criterion holds for groups as well. A community must develop its own inner identity. The central vision of *I and Thou*—that community emerges from and around a common living center—is used polemically and propagandistically here. Only those social movements which have at their core a genuine, living center can be affirmed. Only that social movement whose aim is to realize the inner potential of communal life can be given approval once the principles of *I and Thou* are accepted:

> The feeling of community does not reign where the desired change of institutions is wrested in common, but without community, from a resisting world. It reigns where the fight that is fought takes place from the position of a community struggling for its own reality as a community.[12]

The political criterion on social movements—their success in the arena of institutions and their forcefulness in altering social structures—is replaced by the religious criterion of *I and Thou*: how well does the movement enable the community to develop according to its own internal pattern?

From *I and Thou,* as well, comes the idea of community as a struggle to realize a pattern, to actualize an image held potentially by the group in its relationship to a living center. If institutions are a "golem," a mass of inert clay, then community can arise only as human beings do—from the symbiosis of clay and spirit. The creation of community is as much a work of art as any other struggle with material reality. Social movements are public works of art, a work of art executed in common. The investigation of social life found in *I and Thou* suggests that community is not just man's response to "spirit"—as is all art—but man's response to the Eternal Thou. Community, then, is the first and most important consequence of encountering the Eternal Thou, of experiencing revelation.

Describing community as a response to revelation enables Buber to launch another critique. Community is not merely man's way of making do. It is not merely an expedient measure by which people are kept from devouring one another. The argument that community is instinctive, that it derives from human greed and thrives because of innate human weakness is rejected because of Buber's discussion in *I and Thou*. Marx and Engles were misleading when they rejected "utopian" socialism. Realistic socialism which, presumably, only recorded the inevitable development of human life and society based on inexorable laws of history, economics, and human nature could never, in Buber's view, produce true community. If, as *I and Thou* contends, only living relationship to a common center creates community, then community must have a religious dimension. This dimension suggests that more is at stake in community than a realistic assessment of economic, social, or historical facts could make clear. A vision is at work, an intuition born of reflection on an encounter—that encounter which is itself the hub of community:

> In the history of the human spirit the image-creating wish—although it too, like all image-making is rooted deep down in us—has nothing instinctive about it and nothing of self-gratification. It is bound up with something supra-personal that communes with the soul but is not governed by it. What is at work here is a longing for that *rightness* which in religious or philosophical vision is experienced as revelation or idea, and which of its very nature cannot be realized in the individual but only in human community.[13]

Buber uses *I and Thou* to propagandize his view of community as a religious manifestation. On the basis of this propaganda he can assume a receptive ear for his criticism of the apparently sophisticated realism of Marxism.

While in the first place negative, Buber's social theorizing also advances some positive claims. He demands that community reflect the participation of every individual. He declares that the more politics and government are isolated from such participation the less a society realizes its social purpose. The more the actual practice of communal life is abstracted from the community itself, from the individuals involved, the less possible true communal relationship becomes. Buber demands that community organization be flexible and responsive because without such responsiveness it ceases to be true community: "But the more a human group lets itself be represented in the determination of its communal affairs and the more from outside, so much the less community life exists in it, so much the poorer in community does it become."[14] No one stage in its development can ever be regarded as final. Just because community is made up of dynamic individuals, its own self-organization must be dynamic. Change and growth are the only true reflections of changing and growing persons. Buber points out that the "true history of a commonwealth must be understood as its striving to reach the order suited to it . . . [this] constitutes the political structure's dynamic of order. An order is gained and established again and again as a result."[15] Community must express its politics as an ever new coming to grips with its self. Political dynamics implies just this developing and on-going striving for an order "suited to it." An imposed order, a static political form, a dominant government, all prevent the legitimate dynamics which create and recreate community.

One analyst has identified this restructuring of society as forming "a state of anocracy" in which nondominance is the primary political form.[16] He finds Buber's affirmation of this form a response to modern life in which the person is unconfirmed in his personhood, in which power and technocracy interfere with a self-binding to God. This analysis is accurate but misses, I think, the basic religious concern Buber offers. Buber opposes dominant governments because they inevitably substitute a political center for a religious one. Community arises because of a shared relationship to a single center. Politics provides nationalism, self-interest, or ideology as such a center. Buber finds such provision artificial and destructive. Not political religion but a lived relationship with the Eternal Thou is the center for genuine community; founded centers can only be false ones:

Wherever historical destiny had brought a group of men together in a common fold, there was room for the growth of a genuine community; and there was no need of an altar to the city deity in the midst when the citizens knew they were united round—and by—the Nameless. A living togetherness, constantly renewing itself, was already there, and all that needed strengthening was the immediacy of relationships.[17]

Political power is often demonic because it introduces the unreal, the fantasy, the artificial into that center which provides the only authenticity possible in genuine community. The division between serving God and serving society is a false one, a division introduced by politics itself. In fact, true service of God consists in nothing less than demanding that society become community, community whose center is the true one of the Eternal Thou. "I believe that it is possible to serve God and the group to which one belongs," Buber declares, "if one is courageously intent on serving God in this sphere of the group as much as one can."[18]

Buber defines "religious socialism" as just such a unity of serving God and group: "Religious socialism can only mean that religion and socialism are essentially directed to each other, that each of them needs the covenant with the other for the fulfillment of its own essence." Religion's task is to keep socialism from becoming politics, to remind social theory that persons rather than structures are essential. Speaking of Gandhi, Buber offers a distinction between religion and politics: "Religion means goal and way. Politics implies end and means."[19] Religion enables socialism to maintain its dynamic quality: "Socialism can never be anything absolute. It is the continual becoming of human community in mankind."[20] A basic religious task, then, is to strengthen community, to keep social theory flexible, alive, related to its true center.

If the task of religion is to keep social thought alive, what is the task of the social thinker? Buber contends that such a thinker is "not a prophet but a philosopher. He does not have a message, he has a teaching." We have seen before that a "teaching" implies that the human life is the ultimate realization of the "spirit" conveyed by a form. The social thinker becomes involved in the forms of society in order to point to a particular way of living. The basic message of such a thinker lies in who he is rather than in what he says. His actions, his commitment to social change testify to a belief about human potential. Buber's social writings are addressed to persons, not governments. They call forth a responsive life rather than a political program. The social thinker has been impelled by "spirit" to create a social work of art, but like all true art its true audience is an individual and his personal living. Buber's commitment to the social art form arises from his sense that person and society cannot be separated: "Man must change himself in the same measure as the institutions are changed in order that these changes may have their expected effect."[21]

The basic categories of *I and Thou* have become through this development a life-plan. *I and Thou* posits true community as the gathering of individuals who have a living relationship with a vital center while also being creatively related to each other. Buber as a social theorist uses this insight to demand that social thinking concentrate first on the center around which community is to be built. Inauthentic, artificial, political centers must be rejected. The social thinker, then, has a religious duty: to unmask the idolatry which would replace the genuine communal center—The Eternal Thou—with a human contrivance. *I and Thou* stresses growth, development, and change. Buber as a social thinker refuses to let social structures be frozen into absolutes. Community is a group striving to realize its true self. Such striving implies that change must be accepted as a legitimate part of social life. *I and Thou* precedes this social thinking as a herald preparing the way for a royal procession. The foundation is laid, the view of life secured, and then the way of life which follows upon these principles is constructed. Since Buber's vision of that way is undeniably social and political, one cannot help but find his abstract philosophy in *I and Thou* a subtle but persuasive political propaganda.

Buber's Zionism: I and Thou in a Jewish Context

While socialists in general could find in *I and Thou* a political program addressed to them, Jews read the work in a more specific context. Buber's Zionist connections could not help but color the way in which many Jews read *I and Thou*. Once again the philosophical work is a polemical and propagandistic prologue. But against whom is he directing his argument? Is it addressed to those like Franz Rosenzweig who felt that Zionism was only a tangential religious concern; or is it focused on those political, practical, and cultural Zionists against whom Buber continually argued? To answer these questions we will turn first to the latter Zionist arguments. If after examining them we find a coherence with *I and Thou* then we must admit that Zionists, rather than those like Hermann Cohen or Franz Rosenzweig who held aloof from Zionism, were Buber's targets—and we can legitimately ask why this was so.

Buber, as one might expect, opposes nationalistic ideology which places survivalism or materialistic success at the center of Zionist strivings. For him Zionism is the fulfillment of the Jewish vision which has at its core "the demand that the people submit its entire life, including its social and political activity, to the will of God, the true king."[22] This approach applies Buber's general criticism of "realistic" socialism to the specific case of Israel. As in the more general critique Buber relied upon his work in *I and Thou*. A Jewish community must emerge from a common relationship to the Eternal Thou just as community in general must. In the case of Judaism, examples from the Bible, the Talmud, and medieval writers help demonstrate this point. Buber, however, is weakest when—as in *On Zion*—he attempts to sketch in the common vision which unites the Jews in community. Such descriptions must, of necessity, be weak and vague because they try to form in words an image which can be realized only through communal living. Just this task of articulating in social structures a relationship to the deity which poets and philosophers have tried to capture in words is the one demanded of the new Israeli society.

Buber is at his best when he opposes those who have differing interpretations of Zionism. His scorn for Ben-Gurion, for example, and other practical Zionists who find in the State of Israel a messianic realization demonstrates his ability to deflate exaggerated claims. Buber continually refers to the biblical vision and compares the tensions and strains in Israeli society, and more particularly in the relationship between Jew and Arab, to that vision. If Zionism has meaning it is as a social solution to the human problem of the Jews: how to live meaningful and holy lives in the modern world. Maintaining secure borders, making political alliances, demonstrating military power are perhaps necessary means to this end. Yet Buber doubts that means can be separated so completely from final goals. These doubts lead him to question whether the political and military victories of the Israeli state have really fulfilled the vision which motivates a living Jewish community, the biblical dream. "This quasi-Zionism," he remarks, "which strives to have a country only, has attained its purpose."[23] Buber rejected this view and made spiritual and religious demands of Zionists. A renewed political life for the Jewish people was but a beginning, it provided only the framework for a revived Judaism. The organizational structure of Judaism would remain empty if it did not house a vital Jewish community. Not merely Jewish community but all human community, as Buber pointed out in *I and Thou,* depends upon a living relationship to God. If Zionism were to successfully rebuild Jewish community it would provide an example for mankind. Israeli society in all its crass reality became for Buber the arena in which the creative renewal of community would take place.

Given this vision, how could Buber accept the blatant secularity of Zionism? One answer of course is that he didn't; he stood against the purely political understanding of the move-ment. A second answer, however, is that Buber refused to let traditional religiousness define what he meant by a "living relationship to God." The atheist who is fully engaged in the task of building community, who works for a common goal born out of responsiveness to a living Thou, is acting religiously. Modern man is in crisis not merely because he "does not believe in God," but also because he does not know how to believe in God. The religious crisis of secularization, of loss of belief in God, will not be solved by theology but by the creation of community. Through community individuals discover their commitment to a Thou and upon reflection can acknowledge the presence of the Eternal Thou. Without this I-Thou relationship, however, all talk about theology is useless. A revival of faith, then, must begin with a revival of community; Zionism begins with this latter and so, Buber feels assured, will lead to the former:

> Contemporary Jewry is in the throes of a serious religious crisis. It seems to me that the lack of faith of present-day humanity, its inability truly to believe in God, finds its concentrated expression in this crisis of Jewry. . . . The true solution can only issue from the life of a community which begins to carry out the will of God, often without being aware of doing so, without believing that God exists and that this is his will.[24]

The Zionist movement need not see itself as religious to be effecting God's will. As long as its goal is that of community, as long as a central vision and living connection to that vision characterize its activities, Zionism is working for the fulfillment of God's plan.

This visionary ideal of Zionism was threatened by various false images of Zionism as purely political or as a self-interested attempt to develop Jewish power. Buber recalled that when he entered the Zionist movement the burning issue was the choice between "practical" and "political" Zionism. The first sought a slow, gradual building of the land. Political independence could come, according to this view, when the process of growth and development had matured. The second view, characterized by the leadership of Theodor Herzl, sought a dramatic political victory which would create the Jewish state in one decisive act. Buber remarks that "I decided without hesitation" for practical Zionism.[25]

Political Zionism approached its task from the outside. First create a political structure, then seek to fill it with Jewish life.

113

Buber's view saw in Jewish life the constructive force building the political structure. External salvation in Buber's mind was indelibly associated with apocalyptic and messianic movements. While the prophet speaks out of a genuine meeting with a genuine Thou, the apocalyptic writer seeks to coerce the Thou. Buber remarks on the fact that when Herzl learned about Sabbetai Zevi, the notorious seventeenth century false Messiah, he responded that Zevi had failed because he lacked machines. Buber noted that Zevi and Herzl were seeking the same ends and then commented that Herzl would fail as had Zevi since "not machines but the power of authentic faith will decide the ultimate success of the Zionist work of settlement."[26] Buber's Zionism spoke out for the faith that springs from community and against the political approach which identified communal life with institutions.

A danger common to both practical and political Zionism, however, was that of making the nation and national ideology an end in itself. Buber's Zionism saw the Israeli community as more than an expression of Jewish identity; it was the beginning of mankind's rediscovery of I-Thou. He spoke against practical Zionists when they made expediency rather than relationship the basis of their activities. "National ideology, the *spirit* of nationalism," Buber maintains, "is fruitful just so long as it does not make the nation an end in itself." When practical Zionists began to create their vision by exploiting the Arabs in the land, Buber raised his voice in protest. Such actions reveal an I-It rather than an I-Thou approach to nationalism. "Our *historical* reentry into our land took place through a false gateway," he laments. True community extends to all who share commitment to the central vision, not only to a select ethnic group. The task of the Zionist which Buber sets is to "seek to free once again the blocked path to an understanding with the Arab peoples."[27]

The social visionary recognizes the limits of his power. He must distinguish between the possible and the not-yet possible. "The personal responsibility of the revolutionary," Buber declares, "is, according to its nature, one of demarcation."[28] In his approach to the Arab people Buber is drawing such a distinction. At one time the task may have been to create community with the Arabs; now the task is that of opening the path. But how can Buber be sure that there is a path, that a road lies ready to be opened? His response is that such is the destiny of the Jewish people, such is the Judaic vision. Israel, for Buber, "was and is a people and a religious community in one. . . . He who severs this bond severs the life of Israel."[29] Buber points out the possible and the not-yet possible; beyond this he points out that the existence of the people of Israel depends not merely on what is possible here and now but precisely on what is not-yet possible.

To whom was Buber addressing his message? As first glance it seems that he spoke to those Zionists who glorified success, political victories, and military might. Yet on second glance we notice that his major concern was with setting up boundaries, with determining when and where it was imperative to act and when and where the individual had to withdraw into abstract thought. The principles of *I and Thou* lie just below the surface in all these Zionist writings; presumably Buber expected his readers and auditors to have a sympathetic response to that general theory. He was, then, speaking to those who found in his religious approach a valid way of looking at the world. Seen from that perspective, *I and Thou* takes on a different meaning in relationship to Buber's Zionism. It is the preparation which precedes Buber's entrance into the political arena; *I and Thou* explains why such political concerns are valid and legitimate. Because of *I and Thou* Buber's writings on Zionism can be addressed to a wider circle of readers.

I and Thou is subtle Zionist propaganda directed at those who are indifferent or even hostile toward the Jewish national movement. Its premises demand that society be taken seriously. The individual is challenged to enter into the social sphere, to take upon himself the task of participating in community. The next logical step is entrance into a natural communal setting. Buber's Zionism makes clear that for the Jew the national movement is just such an opportunity. The philosopher, *I and Thou* suggests, must become involved in social life. Social life,

Buber's Zionist writings demonstrate, is equally in need of the philosopher. When Buber analyzes a Zionist problem he is giving an example of I-Thou social thinking; he is putting the critical stance of his book into action. By so doing he forces those who are intellectually ambivalent toward Zionism to make a personal decision. They must make their own boundary choice. Buber has given evidence that the man of religious commitment is needed by and therefore has a responsibility to the social body.

The major issues of Buber's Zionism are the relationship of ideology and religion, the goals of a nation-state, and the justification of the Jewish return to their homeland. His reconciliation of these issues goes back to his view of social theory. Beyond that, however, *I and Thou* can be interpreted as a hidden answer to just these issues. From *I and Thou* Buber drew the premise that only from community, in the responsive life of Thou-saying, could institutions draw their power. Such a premise already answers the Zionist question of justifying an Israeli state. External forms—laws, precedents, even the biblical "promise"—are insufficient. Only a vital lived relationship with the Eternal Thou and with other men can justify community. Appeal to precedent is of no avail. Only an appeal to vital religious reality is compelling. From *I and Thou* Buber derives his view of community as centered on shared relationships with the Eternal Thou. Such a view already rejects the claims of ideology, nationalism, and survivalism as legitimations for the Jewish state. Such a view also implies that the social thinker must also be a religious thinker, must offer a "teaching" rather than a message. If community is determined by relationship to the Eternal Thou, then social theory is also theory about living in vital response to the Eternal Thou. Religion rather than ideology must be the source of Israel's identity, for without a religious relationship to the Eternal Thou the community has forfeited its authenticity and genuine identity. The basic call of *I and Thou* is for openness to You-saying, both by the individual and through open social structures. As he stated in his early writings, Buber called Jews to Zion as a call to "a community of men who, in the name of the nameless God will journey to Zion of His realization"; certainly these two calls are not only compatible but identical.[30] They differ in language because they are addressed to different audiences; their content, however, is the same.

This discovery should increase an appreciation of the Judaic importance of *I and Thou*. Scattered and infrequent as they are, the social references in *I and Thou* are central elements in Buber's thought. Whether his previous engagement with Zionism influenced these pages or whether it was his religious thinking that determined his subsequent Zionist stance and adversary position, the two are intricately related. *I and Thou* provides a metaphysical foundation for Buber's social activities, a theoretical justification for his practical endeavors. The reader of *I and Thou* who is aware of this symbiosis between Buber's political and philosophical activities finds his reading enhanced. The tract is lifted from the plane of abstract speculation and becomes part of a social polemic. Its message is not merely philosophical but also social and political.

When viewed in this way, *I and Thou* becomes a primary example of a politics which transcends itself and becomes an invitation to encounter. *I and Thou,* as we have seen, is undeniably political, almost propagandistic, for Buber's utopian socialism. And yet all he demands is that the reader respond, that the reader join in an engagement with the center of being, that the reader encounter a genuine other in a genuine community. *I and Thou* is an example of a universal Zion—which is no less Zionistic for being universal. Although its politics remains below the surface, *I and Thou*'s close ties with Buber's Zionist writings make its political purpose clear. *I and Thou* motivates the reader to search for true community, a responsive community engaged with a living religious center. The reader is not far from Buber's intention if he finds such a community in an idealized Zionism. Recognition of this hidden Zionism gives depth to the social message found in *I and Thou.*

Chapter IV

Judaism and Buber's View of God

Buber's view of God is not only philosophically the most developed of his views but also the most controversial. If Buber's I-Thou thinking is rooted in Judaism, then there must be a continuity between his view of God and that of traditional Jewish philosophy and theology. In the introduction we noted that *I and Thou* directs its third part to the problem of *religion*—the human response—rather than to God—the primal stimulus. In that context the questions of freedom, will, idolatry, and theology were viewed as elements in the larger issue of "religiosity." Judaism, however, is far from being theologically indifferent—a mistaken view derived from Moses Mendelssohn's oft misused contention that Judaism has no dogmas. Jewish theology demands a God who reveals his will in Torah, who enters into relationships with men, and who permits men to respond to his call in freedom. Buber, of course, contends that his philosophy is Judaic in just these elements. His interpretation of monotheism, revelation, and human freedom takes up these very issues. *I and Thou* establishes the framework within which traditional Jewish claims can be understood. But while Buber sees his philosophy as Judaic, others do not.

M. Z. Sole gives a critique of Buber's theology. He recognizes that Buber opposes the philosophical approach which reduces God to an idea and the sociological or psychological interpretations that identify God with an institutional, social, or personal function. Insofar as Buber "follows the path of the medievals" and defines God by negative attributes, Sole finds him on solid Judaic ground. But when Buber offers a positive definition of God as the Eternal Thou, Sole disagrees. Such a view is as philosophical and abstract as any Buber has criticized. Such a God is an idea who can neither command men nor enter into relationship with them. Buber, he claims, has presented nothing more than another philosophical reductionism. If God is found only in the phenomenal world, then how can any philosopher grasp his reality? Such a God, Sole concludes, is a "God of the philosophers," and not "a God of the believers."[1]

A more extended critique of Buber's thought in general and his theology in particular is given by Eliezer Berkovits. Berkovits recognizes the centrality of ethics and morality for Buber—human freedom is the foundation upon which I-Thou depends. Yet human freedom and the ethical choice, Berkovits maintains, depend on public action for their validation, and the private, almost secret, nature of Buber's dialogical situation undermines the public reality of human behavior. I-Thou meeting can be reduced to subjective experience since the external reality of others depends upon *public,* or general, knowledge. Given the subjective aspect of I-Thou meeting Berkovits claims that "Dialogical revelation cannot provide the quality of absoluteness in ethical values and moral obligations."[2]

The issue is crucial. Buber claims that the one obligation is a readiness to step into I-Thou relationship. All extrinsic obligations can fall into I-It institutionalization. I-Thou, however, generates a sensitivity to the Thou which, on reflection after the encounter, leads to specific ethical actions. If by obedience to the "grand will" Buber means only a willingness to enter into relationships and no specific ethical content, then Berkovits claims Buber has trivialized God's role in ethics and created a relativistic ethical system. "The absoluteness of ethical obligation," he comments, "has its source in the absolute will of God revealed to man as His law. Without content in revelation, all ethical obligation is relative."[3]

Buber, of course, claims that an absolute law stands in the way of responsiveness. Detailed laws prevent I-Thou encounter and make men deaf to God's voice. Berkovits argues that this emphasis on a personal hearing of God's voice is religiously unacceptable. "Even if God remained forever silent for him, the man of faith would call again and again and would know that he was heard." Buber would reply that the essence of meeting with God is not a one-way street in which one "is heard," but an encounter in which relationship is made possible. Berkovits and Buber are divided precisely at this point. Buber claims that ethical choices are made freely in response to demands arising from I-Thou encounter. Berkovits sees men as trapped by ethical weakness and personal flaws. Meeting God, man does not learn his strength, but his helplessness: "Far from entering into a relation of mutuality in the encounter with the Divine, man becomes aware of his utter helplessness in the presence of God." Buber supports his view of the Eternal Thou by making relationship to the other a basic prerequisite of personhood. Because without encounter even the Eternal Thou loses its personhood, God needs man just as man needs God. Berkovits is led to question the Judaic authenticity of this view. Buber's thinking, according to Berkovits, has led from a subjective ethics, to an affirmation of strength in the presence of God, to a final hubris—the declaration that God needs man: "The idea that in the pure relation man experiences himself as a creaturely creator needed by God is so foreign to the biblical encounter that it starts one wondering whether Buber's I-Thou is indeed a genuine confrontation between man and his creator."[4]

Both Berkovits and Sole have criticized Buber's view of the Eternal Thou as being un-Jewish. Both have advanced theoretical and philosophical arguments to demonstrate that the Eternal Thou is a philosophical construct and not a religious statement. Yet the perceptive reader of *I and Thou* will notice that the third section, the section concerning theology, is focused more on religion and the issues of religion than on a philosophical understanding of God. Buber's major concern is how the Eternal Thou is met and then perverted by religious traditions. Before turning to Buber himself, then, we should look at his critics. Although Sole does not spell out his religious presuppositions, Berkovits provides his reader with certain positive statements about Jewish religious life. These statements describe the foundation of Berkovits' Judaism and the basis on which he criticizes Buber. Three major contentions stand out as being of primary concern: the Jew who believes in God also believes that God must give him a specific law; the Jew who takes God's creation of man seriously must take his self-definition from that given him by God; and finally, free will is exercised in the act of interpreting the law, not in the act of accepting or rejecting it.

"A faith in God that leads to the deed in the presence of God asks for a law of God," Berkovits declares.[5] Such a declaration stands in flagrant contradiction to Buber's call for responsive deeds unfettered by law. The traditionalist sees God's unity and power translated into a uniform and absolute law. If God is real and his unity real, then too his demands must be uniform and unchanging. Buber objects to such a religiousness as idolatry. It sets up a human construction as a straitjacket for God. For Buber, the demand of monotheism to recognize the unity of God is a rejection of pantheism rather than the basis for an absolute legalism.

What about morality? Isn't an absolute law needed to give the moral imperative its force? Berkovits locates such an absolute claim in the belief that man was created by God and is thus God's creature. This view leads, according to him, to recognition that God alone defines man's being: "Such is the nature of human subjectivity that it can realize itself only by taking due cognizance of the objectively given reality that is God."[6] Man must allow God's sense of man to determine his objective status. Buber agrees that in revelation man discovers himself, but denies that man can "take cognizance" of that revelation. To meet Berkovits' criticism Buber will have to show that even in a "contentless" revelation men discover the essence of personhood and that although they are equal partners such discovery would have been impossible without God.

Finally Berkovits argues that in Judaism freedom of the will is an important element—but in determining the application and interpretation of the law, not in accepting or rejecting it: "The form is objective; the meaning of its contents is subjectively

121

directed to each man in his time."[7] (Buber's emphasis on will as waiting complicates this Jewish approach.) Buber would reply that man's "puny will," his self-interest, is at work in such legalistic willfulness. To establish his claim against Berkovits, Buber must show how the working of the "grand will" is equally an act of moral decision-making.

Buber's interpretation of God has been challenged in terms of its philosophic abstractness, its moral flexibility, its hubris. These criticisms reduce to the opposition of a structured, content-filled revelation to a responsive contentless revelation. The three major issues are those of Buber's view of monotheism and idolatry, revelation, and the human will.

Monotheism and Idolatry: Buber's Response to Pantheism

Again and again Buber comments that our concerns must be "not for the other side but for our own, not for grace but for will." What does religion mean by monotheism; how does that effect change human behavior? On the one hand thinkers like Berkovits claim that monotheism implies one absolute law for human action. Buber begins with the encounter with the Eternal Thou. Such an encounter does not limit but rather expands human choices. While unconditional exclusiveness is present, unconditional inclusiveness is there as well.[8] Berkovits and those like him base their argument on a true intuition. There is an exclusive, absolute demand issuing from the contact with God. But this is not a unified, absolute law. Such a law is made impossible in a meeting with the Eternal Thou.

What does such a meeting imply? In the first place it implies that all aspects of life have meaning. The world—in all its variety—is validated. Secondly, all relationships—with other people, other things in the world, other ideas—"become transfigured 'in the countenance of God.' "[9] The absolute morality derived from God's presence is that attitude which sees all others as creatures, as partners, as equally present to the Eternal Thou. Such a morality is absolute and binding, as binding as any detailed law. On the other hand it makes a detailed law impossible because such a law is by its nature partial and limited. Detailed ethics are always I-It reflections on the sense of divine value with which the I-Thou encounter has invested all of life. That encounter is by its nature pluralistic—legitimating the variety of life's expressions. Law by being I-It manipulation of life's forms is necessarily limited and restricted.

If the I-Thou relationship does not provide one common moral code but rather a pluralistic response based on one general moral imperative, then does it make sense to speak of monotheism? Why speak of one God if his expectations are so varied? Buber interprets the unity of God to indicate "the exclusiveness which rules over the faith-relation as it rules over the true love between man and man."[10] Monotheism is an injunction to approach God freely, without the mediation of a law. Monotheism means that we meet God only by taking the other seriously as a partner in relationship. From this standpoint the idea that man only meets God in his law is a perversion; monotheism means meeting God as a Thou.

Of course Buber admits other interpretations of "monotheism." He explains that not the name but the actuality is crucial: "Within the so-called Monotheism the concrete difference of the images of God and the vital relationship which shapes all other relations with God," Buber comments, "made incisions which are sometimes far more important than the boundaries between a particular 'Monotheism' and a particular 'Polytheism.' "[11] Monotheism means for Buber not merely affirming one God but affirming that every human activity is directed to one sanctified purpose. The Egyptian king Akhnaton reduced the Egyptian pantheon to one supreme God. Such a move was not, according to Buber, Judaic monotheism because it lacked concrete realization in everyday Egyptian life. Monotheism is not a statement about God's reality but about man's relationship to God and through that relationship to the world.

The same type of distinction between "monotheisms" appears in Buber's contrast between Jesus and Paul. Jesus together with the Jewish tradition does not find God invisible, impenetrable, and beyond human reason. The Synoptic Gospels show that Jesus, like the Jewish tradition in general, was distinguished not "by a more spiritual view of the Godhead, but by the exclusiveness of his relationship to his God and by his reference of all things to Him." Pauline Christianity and John's Gospel "spiritualized" faith and rarefied divinity beyond human comprehension. By making God's reality a mystery such Christianity may have refined monotheism, but for Buber it lost the concrete consequences which validate any monotheism. Whereas Jesus demands that Jewish law be performed with love, "even love, the fulfilling of the law, is not valid for Paul as fulfillment of the law, but only when it is through faith in Jesus as the Christ."[12] Even if God is numerically one, Buber suggests, if human actions can be made ultimately relevant only through an intermediary then Jewish monotheism has been abandoned.

Not only intermediaries but the division of the world into two spheres—the holy and the profane—is for Buber a sign that Jewish monotheism has been deserted. Israel's deity "could not acknowledge any domain in the universe or life, on which he set foot, remaining outside his sway."[13] Such a God is to be recognized by an enduring personality penetrating the various guises of life and nature.

The division of the world into two spheres reminds us of the intricate laws of purity and impurity, of forbidden and permitted actions, of holy and profane hours, found in traditional Judaism. Buber suggests that the view which associates belief in God with the necessity of accepting his law has introduced plurality into true monotheism. The legalism of a Berkovits is in fact idolatry—it has set up a secondary reflection stimulated by a true I-Thou encounter as the totality of revelation. Idolatry is not merely worshiping the true God under a false name; it is accepting the name (or in this case the law) of God as exhausting God's actuality or (in this case) the implications of his presence for human action. Any name of God is sacred, according to Buber, because it not merely describes God but is a means of addressing him.[14] When a mode of address is taken as a total description it becomes idolatrous.

The legalist thinks that he possesses "God." He knows all

that God requires of him; he can "take cognizance" of God's view of man; he can know which parts of life God intrudes in and from which he is excluded. Such a characterization may be unfair to Berkovits, but Buber's cry, "Woe unto the possessed who fancy that they possess God," can apply to those who believe they have received the full meaning of divinity in a humanly conceived and transmitted tradition.[15] The traditionalist attends to God's needs, performs his required tasks. In so doing he inevitably uses second-hand reflections. I-Thou encounter generates no concrete deed. To accept such concrete legislation is to set up as absolute another human being's afterglow from an I-Thou meeting. Such an approach perverts the essence of an encounter with the divine. In that encounter the human being finds himself enabled to converse with God but unable to "attend" to him:

> When you are sent forth, God remains presence for you; whoever walks in his mission always has God before him; the more faithful the fulfillment, the stronger and more constant the nearness. Of course, he cannot attend to God but he can converse with him. Bending back, on the other hand, turns God into an object.[16]

Berkovits suspects Buber of misleading his readers. Can the Eternal God whose names are many and whose forms are varied be a partner, a true other? Can one converse with such a deity? Berkovits, Buber might argue, has missed the distinction between conversation and attention. Man's relationship to God always includes a rededication to action, an expanded sense of duty. A man turns from this relationship to the world with a renewed sense of its possibilities for relationship. Man is assured that his efforts to transform I-It existence into I-Thou encounter are not solitary and isolated but grow from his conversation with the Eternal Thou. Any specific command would be a limitation of the general assurance which Buber associates with monotheism. Such restriction of God's concern refutes the basic content of man's meeting with God: all of life can, and therefore must, be hallowed. The particularization of God as this or that absolute inevitably leads to a corruption of monotheism: "But a man's relation to the 'particular something' that arrogates the supreme throne of his life's values, pushing eternity aside, is always directed toward the experience and use of an It, a thing, an object of enjoyment."[17] Relationship implies man's response rather than the individuality of the other. Because God stimulates man's hallowing of the whole of life, God can be described as one. Because precisely this totality is the object of man's activities it cannot be identified with God's presence. God's presence accompanies man as a sense of task, not as a concrete this or that in the world or even expressed by the world. Sole's contention that Buber's God lacks substance might seem cogent. If God cannot be pointed toward without an inevitable objectification, that is to say, if monotheism must avoid any specific designation for God, does God have reality? Buber explains that he cannot help but designate God as person. Only God as person can express man's reaction to divine encounter. God's reality is testified to by man's response. The substance of the divine is manifest in the tasks which men find made possible for them. Only a divine person, only a substantial deity, can explain the mysterious reality of human meetings:

> The designation of God as a person is indispensable for all who, like myself, do not mean a principle when they say "God," . . . all who, like myself, mean by "God" him that, whatever else he may be in addition, enters into a direct relationship to us human beings through creative, revelatory, and redemptive acts, and thus makes it possible for us to enter into a direct relationship to him. This ground and meaning of our existence establishes each time a mutuality of the kind that can obtain only between persons.[18]

Idolatry is that relationship to divinity that prevents encounter by restricting and confining deity to one sphere of life. Idolatry fails to overcome I-It existence because it relegates even the divine to object status. Monotheism represents that religious response which enables men to see all of reality as open to relationship. God, for the monotheist, is that person whose relationship to man has enabled man—and obligated him—to encounter all things in the world as living others. Berkovits is wrong to say that such a view is pantheistic. A meeting with God validates all relationships but is not the sum of them. The world and the self have existence outside of God; they depend on God, however, for their quality of living responsiveness. Sole is also wrong. Since monotheism refers to man's reaction rather than God's substance, one cannot expect Buber to offer a substantial definition of the divine. More than this, Buber rejects such definitions as intrinsically alien to monotheism since they limit the scope of God's concern. God's substantial being, however, is clearly established by analysis of man's response. The possibilities of encounter are inexplicable without reference to a real presence that has been met.

The reality of God and his separate identity from all creation derive ultimately from his revelation. Buber's insistence on God's personhood and on his unique relationship to men stems from his view of the meeting with the divine. One wonders if that revelation is as contentless as Buber sometimes suggests, how it can provide a basis for these claims about the divine. How does that revelation confirm man's reality? What occurs in such a meeting? Is there a sense of obligation connected with revelation, as Buber's Judaic critics would demand? These questions need to be addressed if Buber's identification of monotheism with a unified attempt to hallow all of life, of idolatry with the objectification of God, and of God's reality with the response of man to God's presence can be established. Buber may not be a pantheist, but his rejection of pantheism depends on his interpretation of revelation. We need to explore the meaning of that occurrence.

Revelation and Relationship: Man's Nature as God's Message

Monotheism, we saw, was for Buber a description of the human response rather than of the divine reality in itself. Revelation is also a message about man rather than about God. Although no "content" is conveyed in an I-Thou relationship men do discover a truth about themselves: the truth that relationship and encounter are possible. Just such a truth inheres in revelation: "What is disclosed to us in the revelaton is not God's essence as it is independent of our existence, but his relationship to us and our relationship to him. We can only receive revelation if, when, and so long as we are a whole." Revelation comes to man only when he is whole; it requires a response of the entire man. Revelation as a phenomenon teaches man to need to be whole, to be open and prepared for an address: "Nothing can relieve us of the task of opening ourselves as we are, as a whole and a unity, to the continual revelation that can make all, all things and all events in history and in our lives, into its signs."[19]

At its least, therefore, without regard to content, revelation makes demands on man. Such an encounter is itself a call to remain open to further encounters. Recognizing that the demand inherent in revelation stems from its very existence and concerns man rather than God, we can turn to Buber's discussion in *I and Thou*. Buber describes the encounter with the Eternal Thou as an unexpected discovery: "It is a finding without seeking; a discovery of what is most original and the origin." Through meetings and encounters with other men, with nature or with spirit, men find an intimation of the source of relationship. Revelation is a meeting with that source. In that meeting a discovery takes place. "Man receives, and what he receives is not a 'content' but a presence, a presence as strength. . . . Nothing, nothing can henceforth be meaningless."[20] This revelation occurs within and not outside of man's relationship to mundane others. It derives from immediate engagement with the world, not from abandoning it. Yet it points beyond the world to a reality that underlies it and a responsibility placed on men toward that reality, a responsibility that comes from outside. Revelation, thus, is not God's naming himself but a demand for action:

> We have come close to God, but no closer to an unriddling, unveiling of being. . . . We can only go and put to the proof in action. . . .

> This is the eternal revelation which is present in the here and now. I neither know of nor believe in any revelation that is not the same in its primal phenomenon. I do not believe in God's naming himself or in God's defining himself before man.[21]

Revelation sets a task rather than defines a divinity. God's presence reveals man's obligation in the world, and it does so not by delivering a specific content, a set of dogmas, but by unveiling the basis for life's meaning. Revelation, Buber declares, "is a calling and a mission."[22] Here the objection raised by both Sole and Berkovits is met head-on. Buber does see God's revelation in a Judaic way. God reveals a path, an obligation. Yet because, like monotheism, this revelation demands openness, the obligation cannot be particularized. When Buber points out the general dimensions of this obligation, however, his critics once again claim that he has left Judaic tradition. Buber's claim is that man discovers God's need of him. Certainly Berkovits admits that Buber softens his claims in this regard. Nevertheless he contends—and apparently correctly—that Buber places man in the center of his system. Not God's power but human ability to aid God is the primal discovery in the revelational encounter with the divine. The dramatic statement in *I and Thou* is perhaps overly rhetorical but it catches Buber's emphasis:

> That you need God more than anything, you know at all times in your heart. But don't you know also that God needs you—in the fullness of his eternity, you? How would man exist if God did not need him, and how would you exist? You need God in order to be, and God needs you—for that which is the meaning of your life.[23]

Is this content of revelation an un-Judaic hubris? Buber is referring to man's task—encountering the world and others. God needs man to hallow all of life; such is the content of revelation. Man discovers not only that the world can be encountered but that this encounter is possible because God has desired it. Men encounter the world because God has need of such encounters. Revelation confronts man with his ability to satisfy this need:

"for revelation is nothing else than the relation between giving and receiving." Man's task is to aid the creator in his task. As creator God is concerned with the whole of creation; as revealer God wills that man actualize the whole range of experience. Notice, however, that it is God who both creates and reveals. Before revelation men had certainly experienced their ability to encounter. Buber's ontology implies that I-Thou existence is a necessary art of human growth. But revelation is more than I-Thou living. It occurs when men meet the God who enables encounter. In revelation men find the meaning of encounter as a divine meaning. Men learn that they have been empowered to enter into relationship. Such learning brings with it responsibility: "The power God lends a man gives God a claim upon the recipient which he must satisfy with all he does and does not do. Power is, moreover, authorized by God only to the extent to which man uses it in full awareness of his responsibility."[24]

Revelation teaches man that his power of relationship derives from God's presence. Such knowledge renders man in God's debt. The imperative for relationship, then, resides not in things themselves but in God's presence from which man derives the impetus toward encounter. The dialectic between man's ability to enter into relationship and thus fulfill God's ultimate plan for redemption and the fact that it is God himself who confers this ability overcomes both the tendency toward determinism and the exaggerated sense of mankind which critics have pointed out in Buber. Certainly Buber recognized the danger of both extremes. Man's dependence on God could seem to limit human freedom; God's need of man could seem to challenge God's ultimate reality. Revelation for Buber is just that encounter with God as person that resolves the tension between these two poles:

> But the moment of breakthrough in which we experience directly that we are free and yet now know directly that God's hand has carried us, teaches us from out of our own personal life to draw near to the mystery in which man's freedom and God's determining power, the reality of man and the reality of God, are no longer contradictory.[25]

God's power is the reality experienced in encounter together with the equally powerful reality of man's being allowed to enter into relationships. Both man and God are confirmed in revelation.

The two criticisms of Buber's view of revelation find their resolution in this explanation. Critics complain that Buber misses the overpowering nature of revelation. Man is revealed as insignificant and weak compared to the deity. At the same time Buber's contentless revelation is criticized as un-Judaic. Without providing a definite sense of obligation, a revelation cannot be true to the biblical tradition. Buber integrates his response to these two criticisms. In the first place, he does not deny that man realizes his own limited place when confronted by the deity. The deity stands before man as person. Yet for the encounter to take place man must also stand as person before the deity. Where else could this ability to stand as person derive except from God himself? In revelation the Jew recognizes that "In order to speak to man, God must become a person; but in order to speak to him, He must make him too a person."[26] Just this realization places upon man an obligation. Commandment is nothing else but experiencing and responding to the miracle of encounter after recognizing that its possibility is not "naturally" given to man but a gift of God. A human sense of duty derives from that which is beyond both man and nature. God's grace, experienced as encounter, is the basis for that which Buber takes to be the fundamental obligation: an open willingness to encounter the world as an other.

Religion as an Act of Will

Although Buber, as we have seen, remains within the framework of Judaism, he gives a drastic reinterpretation of that tradition. As seen in the first chapter, his basic criterion of vital religiosity is flexibility, openness to change, and dynamic responsiveness. This criterion clearly underlies Buber's view of religious obligation. That obligation arises from a recognition of monotheism: God demands that all spheres of life without predetermination be hallowed. It is reinforced by Buber's construction of revelation: an encounter with the deity that reminds man both of God's power and man's weakness and of man's God-given ability to enter into relationship. From these two newly interpreted religious categories Buber defines religion anew. Religion consists of replacing one's "puny will" with God's "grand will." Religious traditions are guides to revelation and commandment. As such they reinforce the distinction between the man of "capricious will" who allows events and circumstances to determine his thought and the man of "free will" who has accepted the challenge of hallowing all of life. The religious man is one who turns from satisfying his needs to answering the need of God—that is, elevating the world. Puny will is directed toward using and manipulating life; grand will is oriented toward relationship; it waits for encounter:

> Free is the man that wills without caprice. He believes in the actual, which is to say: he believes in the real association of the real duality, I and You. He believes in destiny and also that it needs him. . . . He must sacrifice his little will, which is unfree and ruled by things and drives, to his great will that moves away from being determined to find destiny.[27]

Man's will is twofold as is his mode of being. On the one hand man wills to manipulate and direct things. He longs for security and structure. Just such a will creates idolatry. Men who "possess" religious truths have "willed" according to caprice, according to their own drives and needs. A second type of "willing" is also possible: a willing to wait, to be ready for encounter. Buber calls this the "grand" or "great" will. Man accepts his ability for relationship as an imperative. He wills to be a being who enters into encounters. Buber associates this type of will with religion, saying that "the truth of religion consists not of dogma or prescribed ritual but means standing and withstanding in the abyss of the real reciprocal relation with the mystery of God."[28] Ideas of God, cultic practices, laws and commandments are mere crystallizations of an original freedom. The basic demand is that of utilizing man's potential. Those alternative forms of religious expression which Buber's critics find lacking in his approach to God and revelation are, he would claim, merely expressions of the puny will. The religious person, Buber suggests, recognizes that the constructions of the puny will are false protections from life itself.

Judaism is a religion of living rather than a secure fortress erected against life. I-It existence builds walls and barriers around human living; a religion which serves I-It being erects commandments, rituals, dogmas, and structures which restrict an unfettered, spontaneous response to the divine. Jewish religion, as evidenced by Buber's critics, has often fallen into such a mode. But Jewish religiosity, he contends, is a great call to encounter, responsiveness, and genuine living. The commandments, rituals, and dogmas of Jewish religiosity point beyond themselves into life itself; they provide an entrance into relationship. The religious man is one who sets foot "on the threshold of the sanctuary in which he could never tarry," because the sanctuary itself impels him outward; he is one who never constructs an eternal religious structure but "again and again build[s] houses of worship and human houses in a distinctive conception of space and from a confident soul." The emphasis of the truly religious man is on dynamic and spontaneous response. He is continually rebuilding altars of holiness, homes for life. In contrast those who represent static religion demand a reliable pattern of cause and effect. They cannot risk failure; they are unwilling to forego control and therefore they lack spontaneity. Of such a person Buber remarks that "His world is devoid of sacrifice and grace, encounter and present, but shot through with ends and means. . . ."[29] Not religion and irreligion, but responsiveness and rigid control are the true alternatives before human beings. The religious choice is made by the will; it is not an act of cult or belief but of decision. Buber places the option before the reader—the false security of the puny will or the expectant waiting and genuine response of the grand will.

I and Thou is the presupposition of this view of God and

revelation, a presupposition which renders Buber's view of Judaism more tenable than his critics admit. *I and Thou* legitimates those criteria which Buber uses to select his views on God and revelation from the Judaic theological tradition. *I and Thou* is a document of Jewish faith as much because of its implications for Judaic theology as for its explicit statements. By changing the criterion for religiousness Buber's work in *I and Thou* enabled him to reinterpret Judaism's basic categories. While revelation and monotheism are discussed generally in *I and Thou,* Buber's later works are more specific. What is crucial in *I and Thou* is its view of religion. On the basis of that foundation Buber could expand and clarify the meanings of revelation and monotheism in the biblical tradition. Our analysis of *I and Thou* as a Jewish work is enriched by adding these more explicit musings on revelation and God to the general framework it provides.

Chapter V
Conclusion:
I and Thou and Modern Judaism

Buber's reinterpretation of modern Judaism touched on the major issues of Jewish existence: the meaning of scriptures, the significance of Jewish observance, the goals of Zionism, and the problematics of theology. In each case he applied his general understanding of religious dynamics as explicated in *I and Thou* to a specific Jewish issue. The previous analysis may seem to be top-heavy. Certainly more space is given to Buber's exegesis and his view of Jewish law than to other concerns. Why should this be so? A review of those chapters will show that Buber's exegesis accounts for only part of their content. Contrasting pictures of alternative Jewish approaches make up the balance. Such an emphasis is entirely in place. Buber's efforts on behalf of scripture and Jewish sources were critical even while making original contributions. He took as his task that of rescuing traditional texts from the historical and apologetic writers who had monopolized their usage. He sought to transform these documents from relics of the past into modern messages addressed to modern Jews. The same transformation was the goal of his analysis of Jewish law. He discovered in the past a paradigm of tension between law and spirit, between deed and commandment, between teaching and authority. By making the relevance of that paradigm for modern Jews his primary concern he moved beyond apologetics and historicism. To perform that feat he had to criticize both the radical apologetes such as Franz Rosenzweig and the orthodox defenders of faith such as Samson Raphael Hirsch. Buber's importance, therefore, cannot be separated from the challenges he faced. His own work is inextricably linked with that of others.

Despite presumed antecedents such as cultural Zionism or Rav Kook's mysticism, Buber's approach to Zion is a unique one. His ability to join political and social thinking with a religious orientation stands alone. While he challenged major political figures in Zionism, his theories, as we have seen, were equally addressed to those who were indifferent to Jewish nationalism. Buber's stance in this regard was primarily constructive rather than critical. He broke new ground, clearing a path by which religious values could interpenetrate the political sphere. Buber's theology was equally revolutionary. One cannot discount the influence of Buber's teachers—particularly those sociologically oriented thinkers like Simmel and Dilthey. At the same time, Buber strove to create a new Jewish religiosity. His concern was not so much corrective as creative. Rather than critique views of God, revelation, or human interaction with the divine, Buber evolved his own approaches. In the cases of both Zionism and theological philosophy Buber is best understood in his own terms rather than in tension with or contrast to one or another of his contemporaries.

Seen from the perspective of Buber's engagement with Jewish issues, *I and Thou* expresses both criticism and constructive creativity. It provides the basis on which alternative views of Judaism can be rejected. At the same time it lays the foundation for a new Judaism. The Jewish significance of *I and Thou* can be capsulized as offering the destruction of other modes of interpreting Judaism and suggesting the genesis of a new mode. As we tease out the meaning of this statement we can summarize the foregoing pages and discover the Jewish meaning of *I and Thou*.

I and Thou *as a Critical Force*

I and Thou faces the challenge of modern man's skepticism and sense of history. The problems raised by these attitudes involve Jewish scriptures and Jewish observance. How can sophisticated modern man confine himself to the products of an ancient time? Why should he restrict religious authority to a set of traditionally received texts? Why should he mold his life according to the demands of an outmoded legal system? Buber's contemporaries had wrestled with these questions. Spinoza had suggested that both Jewish law and Jewish scriptures belonged to the past. They held no contemporary significance at all. Certain exegetes drew the obvious conclusion. Agnon's stories show a similar use of past traditions and texts. Leo Baeck hoped to restore the meaning and importance of the past by showing its classical beauty. Both views, however, seemed to lock the meaning of the texts in history. Franz Rosenzweig, however, turned from the past to the present. Texts and laws could be made contemporary. A vital religiousness could flow into the older forms. Certainly Samson Raphael Hirsch would agree. The point of these older forms was that through them living religiosity could flow.

Buber opposed both approaches. Documents from the past could become alive in the present. This presentness, however, was not a recreation of that past but something new and different. Scripture, Talmud, Hasidic anecdote were records of spiritual events; as such records they could stimulate new spiritual events—not recreations of the original event but radical and original events. Law, as well, belonged to the past. Spirit belongs to the present. Between past and present stands the bridge of "teaching." Seen as teaching, Jewish observance is a stimulus to new encounters; teaching is neither recreating the past nor exploring the past but rather living in the present that fulfills—even if it changes—the past.

Buber's response depends upon a rejection of earlier views. Unless both those who historicize Judaism and those who emphasize the present are refuted, Buber's system cannot be maintained. *I and Thou* is the basis of Buber's Judaism because it offers such a refutation. Religiosity, not religion, is the criterion of spiritual life. Freedom for response rather than fidelity to forms or freedom from forms is essential. Without forms, without I-It, life is impossible. Without presentness, without

137

I-You, life becomes unbearable. Given this view of the world both Spinoza and Rosenzweig, Hirsch and Baeck, are insufficient. *I and Thou* permits the modern Jew to find a middle way between regarding Judaism as a relic of the past and as a creation of the present. Continuity and change are both given their place in modern Judaism. Respect for texts and precedents is made compatible with the need for innovation and dissent from precedents. *I and Thou* points out the flaws in either an exclusive past-orientation or a solipsism of self and immediacy. In this way a critical stance is the prerequisite for any modern form of Jewish living.

I and Thou *as a Constructive Pattern*

The modern Jew is faced with dilemmas unknown in the past. How is religion to be integrated with political issues? How is faith communicated to a world that has lost the presuppositions of belief? Biblical and medieval men lived within an integrated cosmos. Politics and religion, belief and life, were part of an organic whole. Modern man's splintered existence rendered the relationship between religion and politics or religion and daily existence problematic. The political Zionist could deny the necessity for any religious basis to his views. The pietest could separate his religious orientation from an involvement in community life: Kierkegaard's lonely knight of faith provides Buber with one example of such thinking. The existentialist philosophers—Heidegger, Jaspers, Sartre—are clearly more aware of man's problems in modern life than the "religious" apologetes—Hirsch, Geiger, Breuer—in the Jewish camp. Jewish orthodoxy concentrated on questions of law, on cult and customs. The nonreligious thinkers seemed to be more concerned with questions of human existence than the theologians. Sociology and psychology offered more to modern man than religious thought.

Buber's response, of course, was that a vital religiosity demanded engagement in the social situation. A religious Jew must enter into Zionist politics and confront the problems of modern existence. Response to God must pervade life: a Jew was being false to his tradition if he hid behind the cult or divorced his religiousness from human suffering. Problems of God's existence, of the meaning of revelation, of man's part in redemption were central ones in a new Jewish religiosity. To be a Jew, Buber explained, was to be involved in the process of making the world holy, of responding to God's need of man. Buber was enabled to transform Judaism into a political and humanistic faith because of his philosophy in *I and Thou*. The discussion of society and community in that book made politics distinctly religious. Community is formed around a holy center; that center provides the framework for I-You relationship. On the basis of this understanding of politics and community, Zionism can be given a religious content. The problem of secularist Zionists or politically indifferent pietists takes on significance. The one is false to the true meaning of society, the other to the authentic religious demand.

On the basis of *I and Thou,* the authenticity of Jewish monotheism and revelation depends less on the acceptance of certain dogmas than on a willingness to encounter the One Eternal Thou. Monotheism and revelation, then, need to be reinvestigated. If they gain authenticity only as expressions and reflections of encounter, then that authenticity must be established. Buber's investigation of God's uniqueness and the meaning of revelation are thereby justified. A truly Jewish concern is focused on monotheism as the reflection of encounter and on revelation as a human phenomenon. Because *I and Thou* transforms revelation into encounter and theology into an analysis of man's reactions to God, Buber could restructure Jewish categories. Without *I and Thou* this reformulation of basic Jewish modes of thought might seem arbitrary. Given the analysis there, Buber's attempts are legitimated.

I and Thou *as the Modernization of Judaism*

What has Buber constructed? A Judaism that accepts and honors the literature of the past, that finds in the legal tradition a teaching which stimulates a life of faith, that gives man dignity and purpose in the face of God and that demands a hallowing of all life including that sphere known as politics. Such a construction of Judaism deserves to be named "modern." It reflects the problematics of scripture which history and critical scholarship have forced on the modern Jew since Spinoza. Such a Judaism also responds to the restlessness with tradition and legal restrictions characteristic of the post-Emancipation age. It acknowledges that authority alone and communal power, even if politically possible, cannot legitimate observance of Jewish practice. The individual and his needs are central to such a Judaism. The decay of organic community is given; the demise of true communal life is the premise of Buber's advocacy of Zionism as a means of restoring community. Modern nationalism is accepted as part of life-experience, even if it needs to be reformed and transformed. The skeptical cast of mind which rejects miracles, a supernaturally authenticated deity, and a historically accurate revelation of God's words is presumed in this Judaism. Buber's Judaism, in short, addresses just that Jew and just that Jewish community which emerged in the twentieth century and faced the specific historical challenge of that century.

As a modern interpretation of Judaism, Buber's Jewish writings need a modern foundation. They need to be grounded in more than the tradition itself. *I and Thou* forms the foundation which enables Buber to use the tradition in a novel way. *I and Thou* is a profoundly Jewish book not so much because its roots are in Judaism but because it points beyond itself to a new Judaism. *I and Thou* indicates those areas of Jewish living which are problematic—interpretation of scriptures, the importance of cult, the religious significance of social life, the meaning of God's relationship to man—with which the modern Jew must wrestle. Discussions of art and spirit in *I and Thou* point to issues of exegesis in Jewish texts; investigation of community and society allow the problems of Zionism to shine through; emphasizing the Eternal Thou as the source of relationship and as in need of man stimulates a reevaluation of basic Jewish theology. One cannot deny that *I and Thou* is far from explicitly Judaic. Yet its dynamics are those of Judaism and the issues it raises are those of modern Jewish religiosity. Given the close association between Buber's general thought in *I and Thou* and the specific way in which he approaches modern Judaism, the two must be seen as intrinsically related, if not on their own terms then in terms of the documentation of Jewish faith. More specifically, *I and Thou* documents the presuppositions upon which a modern Jewish philosophy can be built. Its Judaic significance is that of revealing the foundations of future explorations in Jewish thinking.

Glossary

This glossary has been prepared to help a reader unfamiliar with the many names, terms, and religious traditions to which Buber makes reference. The definitions are short and sketchy and further information should be sought in major encyclopedias on Judaism (for example, the *Jewish Encyclopedia* or the *Encyclopedia Judaica*).

AGGADA: The folklore, miracle tales, homilies, and nonlegalistic material found in *Talmud* and *Midrash,* literature compiled from about the first pre-Christian century to about the seventh post-Christian century.

AGNON, S. Y. (1888–1970): A Hebrew author whose use of *Hasidic* motifs paralleled Buber's. In 1966 he received the Nobel Prize for Literature.

AVOT: One of the chapters or tractates of the *Talmud.* It presents proverbs and sayings by sages living from about the time of Alexander the Great to 210 C.E.

BAECK, LEO (1873–1956): Jewish thinker known for his research on early rabbinic and New Testament writings. A survivor of the Nazi concentration camp Theresienstadt, Baeck expressed a liberal philosophy of Judaism.

BESHT (1700–1760): An acronym made up of the first letters of the words "Baal Shem Tov" (the good master of the name of God).

Buber collected stories about the *Besht,* who is famous as the founder of *Hasidism.*

COHEN, HERMANN (1842–1918): A German-Jewish philosopher who gained reknown as a neo-Kantian. In his later life he turned to Judaism, but as a universalist rejected Zionism. He influenced both Buber and *Franz Rosenzweig.*

DAY OF ATONEMENT: The most solemn holiday in the Jewish year on which pious Jews fast, confess their sins, and spend the entire day in prayer.

DERECH ERETZ: A Hebrew term meaning "way of the world." The Neo-Orthodox Jewish thinker Samson Raphael Hirsch understood the term to mean "the social context" and advocated joining *Torah*—the eternal truths of Judaism—to *derech eretz*—the changing social context.

FRANKFURT LEHRHAUS: Organized by *Franz Rosenzweig* in 1920, this school was dedicated to adult Jewish learning. Buber became director of the school after Rosenzweig.

GREAT MAGGID (1710–1772): The successor to the *Besht.* The name means the "great preacher"; Buber published one of his earliest books on *Hasidism* about the great Maggid.

HAAM, AHAD (1856–1927): The pen name of Asher Ginzberg, the founder of "cultural" *Zionism.* Buber was attracted to Ahad HaAm's ideas but rejected his secularism and reliance upon cultural education alone.

HALACHA: A Hebrew word meaning "way." It is also translated as "law" in contrast to the nonlegalistic *aggada.* It refers to the guidelines given by traditional Judaism to questions of behavior, ritual, ethics, and the like.

HA-MELEKH: A Hebrew word meaning "the king." Buber contends that the prophetic stance is to set *Israel* before "Ha-Melekh," the only true king, God.

HASIDISM: The word means "pietism" and was used together with its related terms Hasid (a pious one) and Hasidim (pious ones) to characterize the movement begun by the *Besht* in Eastern Europe in the eighteenth and nineteenth centuries. The Hasidic leader was called a Zaddik (righteous one) or rebbe (a master).

HERZL, THEODOR (1860–1904): The founder of "political" *Zionism*. Herzl's analysis of anti-Semitism made him feel that the nations of the world would welcome the revival of a Jewish State to solve the "Jewish Question." Buber opposed his political orientation.

HIRSCH, SAMSON RAPHAEL (1808–1888): A leading German-Jewish thinker. He sought to reestablish Jewish orthodoxy by showing its relevance to modern life without compromising its eternal truth. He founded Neo-Orthodoxy which insisted on joining *derech eretz* (modern social life) and *torah* (unchanging religious truths).

ISAIAH: One of the prophetic books in the Hebrew Scriptures. Buber agreed with biblical critics that the book is a composite. The first part he saw as evidence of eighth century Jewish leadership and the last section as illustrative of the concept of discipleship. This section, he suggested, was written by prophets in the Babylonian Exile (sixth pre-Christian century) who reflected on the words of their predecessor in the land of Israel two hundred years before.

ISRAEL: A name given to the patriarch Jacob in the book of Genesis and extended to all his descendants. Thus it is applied to all Jews. Buber uses the term to refer to the Jewish people as a social group. He never means merely the historical kingdom of Israel or the current political State of Israel, but rather the people of Israel no matter how scattered they may be.

JOSHUA: According to the Bible, Moses' assistant who becomes his successor. Buber notes the covenant renewal ceremony which *Joshua* performs after entering the land of Israel (Joshua 24) as an emphasis upon the need to reestablish covenant life again and again.

KOOK, ABRAHAM ISAAC (1865–1935): A rabbinical authority, mystic, and advocate of religious *Zionism*. He became the first Ashkenazi Chief Rabbi of modern Israel and advocated traditional religiousness. He saw in the modern state the beginning of a new flourishing of traditional Judaism.

KORAH: Biblically, a priestly rival to Moses (Numbers 16) against whom both Moses and Aaron finally triumph. In later tradition

Korah became the prototype of all antinomian protests. Buber uses the Korah image to emphasize the necessity for order and authority in social life.

MENDELSSOHN, MOSES (1729–1786): A Jewish thinker of the German Enlightenment who emphasized the separation between Jewish religious ideas and Jewish civil behavior. Judaism, he contended, was a revealed ritual law, but not revealed truth. The Jew could accept, therefore, the ideas and culture of his environment but retain his specific ritualism.

MESSIAH: Jewish tradition expects a personal savior who will inaugurate an age of social and political justice and peace. Buber uses this idea of *messianism* to demonstrate the Jewish search for unity in human social life.

MITZVAH: Commandment, law, or injunction. The Jew has traditionally seen his duties in terms of 613 *mitzvoth,* or commandments, given to him by God. Non-Jews are said to have 7 *mitzvoth* to perform. Buber rejects these views since God, for him, reveals himself but not a law.

MONOTHEISM: The belief in one unique God. Biblical scholars have argued about when this idea arose in Hebrew thought. Many suggest that the idea begins only with Second Isaiah (the writer who lived in the Babylonian Exile). Others trace the idea to Samuel the prophet, to Moses, or to Abraham. Buber rejects these attempts and finds *Monotheism* connoting an approach to life rather than a numerical statement about God.

MOSES: Putatively, the author of the first five books of the Bible. Buber sees in him the formative genius who gave Israel its social structure. Buber states that Moses revealed to Israel laws and observances which enable them to enter into I-Thou encounter.

NABI: A Hebrew word for prophet. The root meaning is "to speak out." Buber interprets it to mean "to set forth" and sees the prophetic task as that of setting alternatives before the people.

ORTHODOX JUDAISM: The traditionalists who insist upon maintaining Jewish law and practice as a God-given pattern of behavior. The term usually refers to those rabbis and authorities in modern times who demand continuity and unchanging loyalty to every detail of Jewish law. *Neo-Orthodoxy* refers to those who give modern explanations of the law and justify traditionalism in modernized terms. S. R. Hirsch represents such a *Neo-Orthodox* stance by affirming the compatibility of modernity and traditional Jewish legal observance.

PASSOVER: The Jewish holiday celebrating the outgoing from slavery in Egypt (see Exodus 1–15, particularly chapter 12). Its celebration includes eating unleavened bread for eight days and holding a *seder,* or evening meal at which the story of the Exodus is retold.

RABBI: A Hebrew word meaning master. It became a technical term of communal leadership after the destruction of the Temple in Jerusalem in 70 of the Christian era. From that time until about 600 these leaders developed the structure of modern Judaism. The literature they wrote included the *Talmud,* works of *halacha* and of *aggada,* as well as the basic Jewish prayers. This literature is called *rabbinic literature.* Jewish leaders from that time on used the title *Rabbi* to designate their authority. In later Hasidism the Hasidic leader was distinguished from the official rabbi by being called *Rebbe* or *Zaddik.*

REFORM JUDAISM: A movement beginning in Germany designed to bring Jewish religiousness into harmony with modern culture. While some of the early leaders in the eighteenth century were moderate in their view of tradition, later leaders rejected the binding force of Jewish law. *Reform Judaism* sought to build an alternative Jewish religiousness to that offered by traditional Judaism. *Orthodox Judaism* in general and *Neo-Orthodoxy* in particular sought to combat Reform.

ROSENZWEIG, FRANZ (1886–1929): A friend and colleague of Buber's. Together they translated the Hebrew Bible into German. He was more positive toward the comandments of Judaism than Buber.

SABBATH: The weekly day of rest in Judaism celebrated by refraining from any labor, activity, or interference with nature. Buber saw in the *Sabbath* a framework for interhuman relationships.

SABBATICAL YEAR: According to the Bible (Exodus 23:11; 34:21; Deuteronomy 15:3) every seventh year the land is to be left fallow and ownership returns to the original owner. Buber interprets this holiday as enabling the Jew to view nature as an independent reality and thereby having I-Thou relationship with it.

SEDER: The ceremony held on *Passover* eve; during the course of a meal a recitation of the history of the Jews in Egypt and their escape is told using biblical and rabbinic materials.

SHECHINA: The Hebrew word for God's indwelling presence. God is present in this world through the manifestation of his spirit, or *Shechina.*

SIMHAT TORAH: Literally, "rejoicing in the law." It refers to the additional day of the eight-day holiday of booths, or *Sukkot.* On this holiday Jews dance with the *Torah* and rejoice in having finished reading it. The new reading begins immediately upon the conclusion of the last book in the *Torah.*

SINAI: Biblically, the mountain on which the law, or *Torah,* was given, also called *Horeb.* As an image in Jewish religion, Sinai means the source of Jewish legalism and all laws are traced back to there—even the latest law is called "a *halacha* from Moses at Sinai." Buber insisted on a "pre-Sinaitic" Judaism, that is, a pre-legalist Jewish religiosity.

SPINOZA, BARUCH (1632–1677): Jewish philosopher in Holland who challenged all revealed religions. Modern Jewish thought begins with attempts to refute Spinoza's view of the Bible.

TALMUD: The name given to the compilation of *rabbinic* writings finally edacted around 600 of the Christian era. It contains primarily legal discussions punctuated by folklore and wisdom sayings.

TESHUVAH: A Hebrew word meaning "return" used to denote "repentance." Buber takes the word in its basic significance to mean turning to God, to wholeness, and to God's world.

TORAH: Literally "the teaching" or "the way." In a restricted sense this means the first five books of the Bible. In Jewish worship these books, written on a parchment scroll, are the central focus. They are placed in a special "ark" and are read from during worship. In a more extended sense *Torah* refers to all Jewish learning from the entire Bible through *rabbinic* literature, including medieval and even modern Jewish thought.

YANIK: An Aramaic word meaning child, or infant. The figure of the *yanik,* or child who can best his elders in religious learning, is prominent in Jewish literature.

YHVH: The four-letter name of God as revealed to Moses at Mount Sinai, or, according to some traditions, in Egypt (see Exodus 3 and 6). Traditional Jews will not pronounce this name. Scholars use it as a designation for the Lord usually when citing specific texts. Buber uses it to refer to God as understood by the prophets.

ZEVI, SABBETAI (1626–1676): A messianic figure who pretended to be able to lead all Jews back to Israel and reestablish the Jewish state. Eventually he converted to Islam and continued his missionary activities under that guise.

ZIONISM: The modern movement to reestablish a Jewish homeland in the land of Israel. Within the movement were many diverse views—cultural Zionists who desired a rebirth of Jewish learning, practical Zionists who desired a slow maturation of the Jewish settlement in Israel, and political Zionists who sought radical political victories. These different views had a common desire—the rebuilding of an independent Jewish community in the lands promised to the Jews by the Bible.

ZOHAR: A book written in medieval Aramaic, with sections in Hebrew, that purports to be a rabbinic text. It is the basic text of Jewish mysticism and exercised important influence on modern Hasidism.

Notes

Introduction

1. Martin Buber, *The Knowledge of Man: A Philosophy of the Interhuman,* edited with an introductory essay by Maurice Friedman, translated by Maurice Friedman and Ronald Gregor Smith (New York: Harper, 1965), p. 169; compare the comments by Walter Kaufmann in Martin Buber, *I and Thou,* a new translation, with a prologue and notes by Walter Kaufmann (New York: Scribner's, 1970), pp. 20, 32, 35; note the criticism found in Baruch Kurzweil, *Facing the Spiritual Perplexity of Our Time* (Hebrew), edited with an introduction by Moshe Scwarcz (Ramat-Gan: Baruch Kurzweil Memorial Foundation, 1976), pp. 73-75.
2. Buber's interest in humanistic psychology finds expression in Buber, *Knowledge, passim.,* in Martin Buber, *Eclipse of God: Studies in the Relation Between Religion and Philosophy* (New York: Harper, 1952). His sociological and anthropological studies demonstrate a consistent concern but are shaped by his psychological interests; see Martin Buber, *Pointing the Way: Collected Essays,* edited and translated with an introduction by Maurice Friedman (New York: Harper, 1957) and Martin Buber, *Between Man and Man,* with an afterword by the author and an introduction by Maurice Friedman, translated by Ronald Gregor Smith and Maurice Friedman (New York: Macmillan, 1965).
3. Buber, *I and Thou,* pp. 32, 35.
4. Martin Buber, *On Judaism,* edited by Nahum Glatzer (New York: Schocken, 1967), p. 3.
5. Martin Buber, *Israel and the World: Essays in a Time of Crisis* (New York: Schocken, 1963), p. 13.
6. Martin Buber, *Hasidism and Modern Man,* edited and translated by Maurice Friedman (New York: Harper, 1958), p. 127.
7. Buber, *Israel,* p. 38.
8. Buber, *On Judaism,* p. 28.
9. Buber, *Hasidism and Modern Man,* pp. 146-51.
10. Buber, *Israel,* p. 33.

11. Buber, *Hasidism and Modern Man*, p. 162.
12. *Ibid.*, p. 166.
13. Buber, *Israel*, p. 158.
14. Buber, *Hasidism and Modern Man*, p. 174.
15. *Ibid.*, p. 176.
16. *Ibid.*, p. 175.
17. Buber, *On Judaism*, p. 138.
18. Buber, *Knowledge, passim; Eclipse*, pp. 78-92.
19. Buber, *I and Thou*, p. 68; Kaufmann continually translates "du" as "You"; however, in the text of this book I will use the more traditional "Thou."
20. *Ibid.*, p. 80.
21. *Ibid.*, p. 89.
22. *Ibid.*, p. 102.
23. *Ibid.*, pp. 123, 127.
24. *Ibid.*, pp. 130, 161.

CHAPTER I: *I and Thou* as a Jewish Hermeneutic

1. Benedict de Spinoza, *The Works of Spinoza*, translated from the Latin with an introduction by R. H. M. Elewes (New York: Dover, 1951), Vol. 1, p. 9.
2. *Ibid.*, pp. 69, 76.
3. *Ibid.*, p. 250.
4. See Nahum N. Glatzer, "Buber as an Interpreter of the Bible," in Paul A. Schilpp and Maurice Friedman, eds., *The Philosophy of Martin Buber* (La Salle, Ill.: Open Court, 1967), pp. 361-80 and James Muilenburg, "Buber as an Interpreter of the Bible," *ibid.*, pp. 381-402. See also Kurzweil, *Facing*, pp. 64-65, 82-89.
5. Moshe Scwarcz, *Language, Art and Myth* (Tel Aviv: Schocken, 1966), pp. 309-32.
6. Buber, *I and Thou*, p. 60.
7. *Ibid.*, p. 61.
8. Buber, *I and Thou*, p. 176.
9. *Ibid.*, p. 92.
10. *Ibid.*, p. 159.
11. *Ibid.*, p. 161.
12. *Ibid.*, p. 124.
13. *Ibid.*, p. 166.
14. *Ibid.*, p. 130. See the discussion by Charles Hartshorne, "Martin Buber's Metaphysics" in Schilpp and Friedman, *Philosophy of Martin Buber*, pp. 49-68. Hartshorne finds in Buber his own philosophy, that of an emerging God whose love of his creatures makes him dependent on them. He admits, "It is my own doctrine which I have succeeded in reading into Buber" but many others blithely assume that Buber holds a "process" theology in which God "grows."
15. Spinoza, *Works*, Vol. 1, p. 90.

16. *Ibid.*, Vol. 2, p. 316.
17. Martin Buber, *The Prophetic Faith* (New York: Harper, 1949), p. 46.
18. Martin Buber, *Moses: The Revelation and the Covenant* (New York: Harper Torchbooks, 1958), p. 77.
19. *Ibid.*, p. 76.
20. Martin Buber, *Kingship of God*, 3d ed., translated by Richard Scheimann (New York: Harper Torchbooks, 1973), p. 63.
21. Buber, *Israel*, p. 97.
22. *Ibid.*, p. 93.
23. *Ibid.*, p. 111.
24. Spinoza, *Works*, Vol. 1, pp. 19, 31, 40.
25. *Ibid.*, p. 54.
26. Buber, *Prophetic Faith*, p. 215.
27. Buber, *Knowledge of Man*, p. 66.
28. Buber, *Prophetic Faith*, p. 2.
29. *Ibid.*, p. 175.
30. *Ibid.*, p. 103.
31. Buber, *Israel*, p. 89.
32. Buber, *Moses*, p. 41.
33. Buber, *Pointing the Way*, p. 200.
34. Buber, *Israel*, p. 98.
35. *Ibid.*, pp. 13, 28.
36. Buber, *On Judaism*, p. 81.
37. Buber, *Israel*, p. 187.
38. Buber, *On Judaism*, pp. 88, 92.
39. For information on Baeck's thought the reader should turn to Albert H. Friedlander, *Leo Baeck: Teacher of Theresienstadt* (New York: Holt, Rinehart and Winston, 1968) and the excellent study of Leonard Baker, *Days of Sorrow and Pain: Leo Baeck and the Berlin Jews* (New York: Macmillan, 1978). Specific references to the personal relationships between Buber and Baeck are found on pp. 88-89, 175-80, and 332-33. In an interesting contrast Baker reports the view that Baeck was a "leader" of German Jewry whereas Buber was a "teacher" of those Jews (p. 176).
40. Buber, *On Judaism*, p. 99.
41. Leo Baeck, *Judaism and Christianity*, translated with an introduction by Walter Kaufmann (Philadelphia: Jewish Publication Society of America, 1964), p. 176.
42. Buber, *On Judaism*, p. 82.
43. Leo Baeck, *The Essence of Judaism*, rendered by Irving Howe based on the translation of Victor Grubenwieser and Leonard Pearl (New York: Schocken, 1948), p. 187.
44. Baeck, *Judaism and Christianity*, p. 189.
45. Leo Beack, *The Pharisees and Other Essays*, introduction by Krister Stendahl, translated from the German (New York: Schocken, 1966), pp. 10-11, 101.
46. Baeck, *Judaism and Christianity*, pp. 139-68.
47. Martin Buber, *On Zion: The History of an Idea*, with a new forward by

Nahum N. Glatzer, Stanley Godman translator (London: Horowitz Publishing Company, 1973), pp. 43, 54-57.

48. Buber, *Israel*, p. 147.

49. Buber, *Hasidism and Modern Man*, p. 24.

50. Martin Buber, *Tales,* p. x.

51. As a characteristic criticism, see Gershom Scholem, "Martin Buber's Interpretation of Hasidism," in *The Messianic Idea in Judaism and Other Essays on Jewish Spirituality* (New York: Schocken, 1971), pp. 227-50 and Rivkah Schatz-Uffenheim, "Man's Relation to God and World in Buber's Rendering of Hasidic Teaching," in Schilpp and Friedman, *Philosophy of Martin Buber*, pp. 403 ff. See also Kurzweil, *Facing*, pp. 66-82, 101-05.

52. *Religion from Tolstoy to Camus*, selected and introduced by Walter Kaufmann (New York: Harper Torchbooks, 1964), p. 425.

53. Buber, *Hasidism and Modern Man*, p. 41; see Scwarzc, *Language*, pp. 216-49.

54. Martin Buber, *The Origin and Meaning of Hasidism*, edited and translated by Maurice Friedman (New York: Horizon, 1960), p. 22.

55. Buber, *Hasidism and Modern Man*, p. 62.

56. Agnon himself gives a stylized account of his relationship to Buber together with a brief discussion of Buber's predecessors in the art of telling Hasidic stories in Shmuel Yosef Agnon, *Me'Atzmi el 'Atzmi* (Jerusalem: Schocken, 1976), pp. 257-72.

57. Shmuel Yosef Agnon, *Kol Sipurav shel Shmuel Yosef Agnon* (henceforth KS) Vol. 8 (Jerusalem and Tel Aviv: Schocken, 1968), p. 90. The best introduction to Agnon is Arnold Band, *Nostalgia and Nightmare: A Study in the Fiction of S. Y. Agnon* (Berkeley: University of Califronia Press, 1968). The bibliography cited there is exhaustive and useful.

58. Martin Buber, *Be-pardes ha-Hasidut* (Jerusalem and Tel Aviv: Mosad Bialik and Devir, 1963), p. 5.

59. See Agnon, KS 2 (*Agunot* and *Agadat Ha-Sofer*) and 7 (*Ha-Malbush*). For translations of the first two tales see S. Y. Agnon, *Twenty-One Stories*, edited by Nahum N. Glatzer (New York: Schocken, 1970). On the theme of unifying the universe and the self and on the imagery of a garment see David Tamar, "Covering and Interior" (Hebrew), in *Le'Agnon Shai*, edited by Dov Sadan and Ephraim Urbach (Jerusalem: the Jewish Agency, 1966), pp. 331-41.

60. Buber, *Origin and Meaning*, pp. 84-85, 126; see also *Hasidism and Modern Man*, pp. 185, 87.

61. *Ibid.*, p. 138; see Agnon, KS 2, pp. 142-43.

62. *Ibid.*

63. Martin Buber, *Tales of the Hasidim*, translated by Olga Marx (New York: Schocken, 1947), p. 17.

64. Agnon, KS 2, p. 506 and S. Y. Agnon, *In the Heart of the Seas*, translated by I. M. Lask (New York: Schocken, 1947), pp. 48-49.

65. Buber, *Hasidism for Modern Man*, pp. 79-80.

66. Buber, *Tales*, pp. 25-26.

67. Agnon, KS 7, pp. 171-77; *Twenty-One Stories*, pp. 252-60.

68. Shmuel Yosef Agnon, *Sifreihem Shel Zaddikim* (Jerusalem and Tel Aviv: Schocken, 1961) is part of a larger work—unavailable to me at

present—focusing on "Books, Writers, and Stories" and this emphasis is clear. Buber's *Tales* are self-consciously chosen to reveal a spiritual "autobiography" of the Zaddikim. Because Agnon's work is in Hebrew it may be best to compare his text with Buber's Hebrew rendering of the tales in Martin Buber, *Or HaGanuz* (Jerusalem and Tel Aviv: Schocken, 1957). Often both Buber and Agnon cite the same original source for their tales, but in checking those sources, when available, I found that both authors had used the texts creatively.

69. Buber, *Or HaGanuz,* front page.
70. Agnon, *Sifreihem,* p. 9.
71. Buber, *Or HaGanuz,* p. 162.
72. Agnon, *Sifreihem,* pp. 13-14; KS 8, pp. 106-07.
73. Buber, *Or HaGanuz,* pp. 76-77.
74. Agnon, *Sifreihem,* p. 10.
75. Buber, *Or HaGanuz,* p. 410; Agnon, *ibid.,* p. 48.
76. Henri Bergson, *The Two Sources of Morality and Religion,* translated by R. Ashley Andra and Cloudesley Brereton with the assitance of W. Horsfall Carter (Garden City, New York: Doubleday, 1935), p. 214.
77. *Ibid.,* pp. 214-15.

CHAPTER II: *I and Thou* and Jewish Ritual

1. See Arthur A. Cohen, "Revelation and Law: Reflections on Martin Buber's Views on Halakhah," *Judaism,* 1:3 (July 1952), 253 ff.; Trude Weiss-Rosmarin, "Judaism and Modern Philosophy: A Review Essay," *Judaism,* 24:4 (1975), 360 ff.; and Donald J. Moore, *Martin Buber: Prophet of Religious Secularism: The Criticism of Institutional Religion in the Writings of Martin Buber* (Philadelphia: Jewish Publication Society of America, 1974), pp. 8-15, and *passim.*
2. Buber, *I and Thou,* p. 150. Although similar to the passage on pp. 56-57, this statement stresses the way men *build* relationships while the earlier one considers discovering them as they "arise."
3. *Ibid.,* pp. 103, 168.
4. Buber, *Prophetic Faith,* p. 164.
5. *Ibid.,* p. 169.
6. Buber, *Moses,* p. 83.
7. Buber, *Prophetic Faith,* p. 55.
8. Buber, *Addresses on Judaism,* pp. 91-92.
9. Buber, *On Judaism,* p. 109.
10. Buber, *On Zion,* p. 15.
11. *Ibid.,* pp. 3-10.
12. *Ibid.,* p. 8.
13. Buber, *Origin and Meaning,* p. 165.
14. Buber, *Prophetic Faith,* p. 70.
15. Franz Rosenzweig, *On Jewish Learning,* introduction by Nahum N. Glatzer, with an exchange of letters between Martin Buber and Franz Rosenzweig (New York: Schocken, 1955), pp. 72-92. Rosenzweig takes Buber's early

addresses as accurate expressions of his mature thought. Although Buber's thought developed and matured, I think Rosenzweig's assumption of a basic continuity of Buber's approach to Jewish law is justified.

16. *Ibid.,* pp. 115, 111, 113.
17. Buber, *Eclipse,* p. 104.
18. Buber, *Israel,* pp. 28-29.
19. Buber, *On Zion,* p. 8.
20. Buber, *On Judaism,* pp. 45-49.
21. See Noah H. Rosenbloom, *Tradition in an Age of Reform: The Religious Philosophy of Samson Raphael Hirsch* (Philadelphia: Jewish Publication Society of America, 1976), pp. 8-13, 135-36.
22. Buber, *On Judaism,* pp. 158-69.
23. *Ibid.,* p. 44.
24. Buber, *On Judaism,* pp. 195-96.
25. *Ibid.,* p. 86.
26. *Ibid.,* pp. 118-19.
27. *Ibid.,* p. 87.
28. *Ibid.,* pp. 150, 44.
29. Buber, *Prophetic Faith,* pp. 171-72.
30. Buber, *Moses,* pp. 187-88.
31. Buber, *Prophetic Faith,* pp. 15-18.
32. Buber, *Origin and Meaning,* p. 160.
33. *Ibid.,* p. 171.
34. *Ibid.,* p. 127.
35. Buber, *Israel,* p. 163.
36. Buber, *Pointing the Way,* pp. 105, 9.
37. Buber, *I and Thou,* p. 163.
38. Buber, *Prophetic Faith,* p. 6.
39. *Ibid.,* p. 205.
40. *Ibid.,* p. 88.
41. Buber, *Pointing the Way,* p. 200.
42. Buber, *Prophetic Faith,* p. 164.
43. *Ibid.,* p. 54.
44. Buber, *Moses,* p. 133.
45. Buber, *Israel,* pp. 142, 140.
46. Buber, *On Judaism,* pp. 168-69.
47. Samson Raphael Hirsch, *Judaism Eternal: Selected Essays,* translated, annotated, and with an introduction and short biography by I. Grunfeld (London: Soncino Press, 1956), Vol. II, pp. 245-52.
48. Martin Buber, *A Believing Humanism: Gleanings,* translated with an introduction and explanatory comments by Maurice Friedman, Credo Perspectives, (New York: Simon & Schuster, 1967), pp. 113-14.
49. Samson Raphael Hirsch, *Horeb: A Philosophy of Jewish Laws and Observances,* translated with an introduction by I. Grunfeld (London: Soncino Press, 1962), p. CLVI.
50. Buber, *Origin and Meaning,* p. 94.
51. Buber, *Kingship of God,* p. 127.
52. Buber, *Prophetic Faith,* p. 82.
53. Buber, *On Judaism,* p. 45.

NOTES FOR PAGES 99-121

CHAPTER III: Buber's Zionism

1. Franz Rosenzweig, *Franz Rosenzweig: His Life and Thought,* presented by Nahum N. Glatzer (New York: Schocken, 1951), pp. 223, 54, 356, 354.
2. Samuel Hugo Bergman, *Men and Ways* (Hebrew) (Jerusalem: Bialik Institute, 1967), pp. 251-52.
3. Buber, *Between Man and Man,* pp. 40-82; *Eclipse,* pp. 115, 120.
4. Buber, *I and Thou,* pp. 155-57, 96, 93, 95.
5. *Ibid.,* p. 94.
6. *Ibid.,* p. 163.
7. *Ibid.,* p. 97.
8. *Ibid.,* pp. 98, 99.
9. *Ibid.,* p. 99.
10. Buber, *Gleanings,* p. 152.
11. Buber, *Between Man and Man,* p. 39.
12. *Ibid.,* p. 31.
13. Martin Buber, *Paths in Utopia,* translated by R. F. C. Hull, introduction by Ephraim Fischoff (Boston: Beacon, 1958), p. 7.
14. Buber, *Gleanings,* p. 87.
15. Buber, *Between Man and Man,* p. 75.
16. Alexander S. Kohanski, "Martin Buber's Restructuring of Society into a State of Anocracy," *Jewish Social Studies,* 34 (1972), 42-51.
17. Buber, *Paths in Utopia,* p. 135.
18. Buber, *Pointing the Way,* p. 217.
19. *Ibid.,* pp. 112, 128.
20. Buber, *Paths in Utopia,* p. 56.
21. Buber, *Pointing the Way,* pp. 190, 179.
22. Buber, *Israel,* p. 258.
23. *Ibid.,* p. 262.
24. *Ibid.,* p. 230.
25. *Ibid.,* p. 253.
26. Buber, *On Zion,* p. 125.
27. Buber, *Israel,* pp. 221, 255, 257.
28. Buber, *Pointing the Way,* p. 118.
29. Buber, *Israel,* p. 249.
30. Buber, *On Judaism,* p. 54.

CHAPTER IV: Judaism and Buber's View of God

1. M. Z. Sole, *Philosophy and Religion* (Hebrew) (Tel Aviv: Augden, 1967), pp. 92-100.
2. Eliezer Berkovits, *Major Themes in Modern Philosophies of Judaism* (New York: Ktav, 1974), pp. 68-137.
3. *Ibid.,* p. 113.
4. *Ibid.,* pp. 118, 107, 109.
5. *Ibid.,* p. 141.

6. *Ibid.,* p. 146.
7. *Ibid.,* p. 147.
8. Buber, *I and Thou,* pp. 124, 127.
9. *Ibid.,* pp. 130, 182.
10. Buber, *Kingship of God,* p. 109.
11. Buber, *Moses,* p. 10.
12. Martin Buber, *Two Types of Faith: A Study of the Interpretation of Judaism and Christianity,* translated by Norman P. Goldhawk (New York: Harper, 1961), pp. 39, 92.
13. Buber, *Prophetic Faith,* p. 40.
14. Buber, *I and Thou,* p. 123.
15. *Ibid.,* p. 155.
16. *Ibid.,* pp. 164-65.
17. *Ibid.,* p. 154.
18. *Ibid.,* pp. 180-81.
19. Buber, *Gleanings,* pp. 113, 114.
20. Buber, *I and Thou,* pp. 128, 158.
21. *Ibid.,* p. 160.
22. *Ibid.,* p. 164.
23. *Ibid.,* p. 130.
24. Buber, *Israel,* pp. 27, 80.
25. Buber, *Origin and Meaning,* p. 103.
26. Buber, *Prophetic Faith,* pp. 64-65.
27. Buber, *I and Thou,* pp. 108-09.
28. Buber, *Pointing the Way,* p. 113.
29. Buber, *I and Thou,* pp. 102, 103, 110.

Index

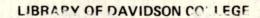